THE USS *TECUMSEH*
— IN —
MOBILE BAY

THE USS *TECUMSEH*
— IN —
MOBILE BAY

The Sinking of a Civil War Ironclad

DAVID SMITHWECK

THE
History
PRESS

Published by The History Press
Charleston, SC
www.historypress.com

Front cover, top: Popular Graphic Arts Collection/Library of Congress, Washington, D.C. Digital file no. LC-DIG-pga-04035; *bottom*: Smithsonian Institution, SIA 2020-002846.
Back cover: Smithsonian Institution, SIA 2020-002845; *inset*: National Archives (NAID 529975).

First published 2021

Manufactured in the United States

ISBN 9781467149747

Library of Congress Control Number: 2021943423

Notice: The information in this book is true and complete to the best of our knowledge. It is offered without guarantee on the part of the author or The History Press. The author and The History Press disclaim all liability in connection with the use of this book.

To Susie, Dave and Charlotte

Battle of Mobile Bay, pencil sketch by Xander Smith. *The Mariner's Museum.*

Battle of Mobile Bay, Xanthus Smith, Pencil Sketch, circa 1864. The Mariners' Museum and Park.

1. Fort Morgan
2. Monitor Manhattan
3. Brooklyn
4. Octorara
5. Tecumseh
6. Flag Ship Hartford
7. Metacomet
8. Richmond
9. Port Royal
10. Lackawanna
11. Seminole
12. Monongahela
13. Kennebec
14. Ossipee
15. Itasca
16. Oneida
17. Galina

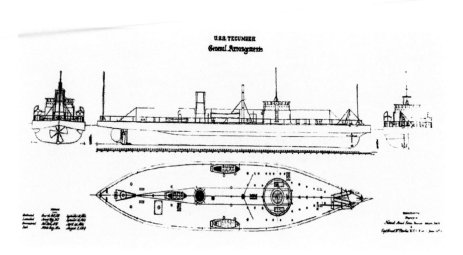

USS *Tecumseh* General Arrangements. *National Archives*.

Also by David M. Smithweck:

Historic Cannons of Mobile, Alabama
Mobile Point Lighthouse, Fort Morgan, Alabama
Lt. Colonel Charles Duval Phillips, C.S.A.
Fort Bowyer: Defender of Mobile Bay, 1814–1815
In Search of the CSS Huntsville *and CSS* Tuscaloosa
Mobile Bay Bar Pilots

Father Abraham J. Ryan, Confederate chaplain. Father Ryan's Poems, *1879, Spring Hill College.*

Nay, Peace! Not so!
The wildest waves may feel thy sceptre's spell,
And fear to flow,
But to and fro,—
Beyond their reach lone waves on troubled seas
Will sink and swell.

—Father Abram J. Ryan, 1879
Chaplain of the Confederate States of America

CONTENTS

Preface   19
Acknowledgements and Preliminary Notes   23

1. *Tecumseh*'s First Assignment   29
2. *Tecumseh* Joins the Gulf Blockading Squadron   35
3. Torpedoes   43
4. The Forts   49
5. Personal Observations: The Fog of War   57
6. Commander Profiles   63
7. Newspaper Press Reports   73
8. 1967 Smithsonian Institution Survey and Dive Notes   81
9. Recovered Artifacts   103
10. Subsequent Surveys   109
11. Other Salvage Attempts   117

Summary and Conclusions   125
Appendix A   127
Appendix B   131
Appendix C   137
Notes   139
Bibliography   147
Index   155
About the Author   159

August 5, 1864, Fort Morgan under siege by Farragut's fleet of four iron monitors and fourteen wood warships. *Popular Graphic Arts Collection/Library of Congress, Washington, D.C. Digital file no. LC-DIG-pga-04035.*

Wisdom from the Civil War
Navy Sequential Memorial,
The Daybook, Special Edition: Technology

*The man who goes into action in a wooden vessel is a fool,
and the man who sends him there is a villain.*
—*Admiral Sir John Hay, 1861*

*Wooden ships may be said to be but coffins for their crew, but the speed of the
former, we take for granted, being greater than the latter. They can readily choose
their position out of harm's way entirely.*
—*Ironclad Board, 1861*

Let not your hearts be troubled: ye believe in God, believe also in the gunboats.
—*niece of Rear Admiral Andrew Foote, 1862*

*I have plans to convert a steamer into a battering ram and enable her to fight not
with guns, but with her momentum.*
—*Charles Ellet Jr., 1855*

*It is my plan to head straight for Cumberland and ram her, for she is the only one
with rifled guns.*
—*Commodore Franklin Buchanan.*

Get under way and close in upon the Confederate monster and destroy it!
—*Admiral David Farragut's order to attack CSS* Tennessee, *1864*

PREFACE

Since the 1600s, wooden warships conducted sea warfare using smooth-bore, iron-shot cannon and large numbers of ships in a line of battle. However, the industrial advancements in the 1800s changed not only the tactics but also the propulsion of steam vessels. Swedish-born engineer and inventor John Ericsson was the architect of many changes with many patented inventions. With the USS *Monitor*, he created the first generation of American ironclad warships. The innovation of large explosive shells capable of annihilating wooden ships changed the Monitor-class design to a low-freeboard, turreted, ironclad one. Iron plating of these new warships was a necessity. The term *railroad iron* became part of the equation, due to the many foundries, in both the North and South, that could supply the shipbuilders. According to the lead professional diver on the *H.L. Hunley* recovery project in 2000, "We found scrap pieces being used in the bilge of *Hunley* as excess ballast." In his navy report, he asserted that these mysterious ingots were likely taken from scrap leftover from the plating of nearby ironclads at the time.[1] This leads me to believe that some of the railroad iron mentioned throughout this period refers to the flat, rectangular iron plates that held the track in place by the use of a spike driven through the plate into the crosstie.

Two major rolling mills were located in the South. The Atlanta Rolling Mill, constructed in 1858 by Lewis & Schofield, and Tredegar Iron Works in Richmond produced the majority of the Confederate iron plating for the South's ironclads. These mills rolled out old railroad rails plus cannon, iron rail and two-inch-thick sheets of iron. Because of the scarcity of iron to make two-inch plates, T-rails from railroad iron were used; but the T-rails were not as protective as the two-inch plating. In the North, the two most productive mills were located in the Chicago area. The North Chicago Rolling Mill Company grew from two hundred employees to one thousand in 1863, and the Union Rolling Mill Company had six hundred workers in 1863.

At the beginning of the Civil War, new innovations dictated the change to ironclad vessels. Fifty-one Union monitors were produced by the United States and thirty-one by England. In 1861, Secretary of the Navy Gideon Wells stated, "I would recommend the appointment of a proper, competent board to inquire into and report in regard to a measure so important; and it is for Congress to decide whether to decide on a favorable report, they will order one or more ironclad steamers or floating batteries to be constructed with a view of perfect protection from the effects of present ordnance at short range and make an appropriation for that purpose."[2] Congress appropriated $1.5 million for construction of the vessels.

Tecumseh is famous not just because of its historical significance in the Battle of Mobile Bay, but also, "as a monitor type vessel, she is important as a specimen of the transition between the wooden fleets of old and the modern navies of today."[3] This was not achieved without a great struggle on the part of traditionalists of the "wood floats, iron sinks" school. Eventually, they were forced into silence by the progress made by ironclad warships.

Maybe the most important aspect of the vessel is that it still has the original equipment just as it was when it went down on August 5, 1864. This presents a unique opportunity to find and explore a historic time capsule.

In the black mud, thirty feet beneath a yellow buoy just two hundred yards off Fort Morgan on the eastern shore of Mobile Bay, lies the Canonicus-class, 2,100-ton iron monitor USS *Tecumseh*, built by the Charles A. Secors & Company, Jersey City, New Jersey, at a cost of $460,000. Francis Secors built Robert Fulton's first two steamboats and signed the contracts for *Tecumseh*, *Manhattan* and *Mahopac* on September 15. The *Tecumseh*'s keel was laid on October 8, 1862, by subcontractor Joseph Colwell at his New Jersey shipyard, and the vessel was commissioned after a long and complicated construction in April 1864.

Designed by Swedish American engineer John Ericsson, *Tecumseh* was 225 feet in length; 43 feet, 8 inches at its extreme width; measured 190 feet from stem to stern; had a 13⅓-feet depth of hold; and had a draft of 12 feet. The aft part of the deck projected some 24 feet, but the forward overhang was only 9 feet. The keel was fashioned from iron plates 18 inches wide and ¾ inch thick, flanged into a hollowed-out gutter 4 inches deep in the center. Every 9 feet, the keel plates were strapped and bolted. The wheelhouse was thoroughly riveted throughout its entire length, and the stern was of forged iron 3 inches thick and 9 inches deep. The turret is 22 feet in diameter with a height of 9 feet. The interior of the turret space was cramped, with room for only two people. The hull is wrought iron, and the deck of 1½ inches of white pine planking is supported by 12-inch-deep by 16-inch-wide wooden beams covered with iron plating. Two boats on two sets of crane davits are located aft of the turret.[4]

It had two independent steering systems and a four-blade propeller of cast iron 14 feet in diameter with a 20-foot pitch. The propeller shaft was a tapering, wrought-iron tube that averaged 15 inches in diameter, and the sternpost was forged from stock 4 inches thick and 9 inches deep.

Two one-thousand-horsepower, vibrating-lever, type-two cylinder engines of Ericsson's design (patent no. 4317) provided the vessel's power. Each of the two cylinders was 48 inches in diameter, and a 24-inch stroke was imparted to the right-angle cranks. The engine could also be reversed. John Dunham & Company and Atlantic Steam Engine Works of Brooklyn received the subcontract to build its four boilers: two main boilers with six furnaces each and two auxiliary boilers with one furnace each. The boilers were arranged side by side. *Tecumseh*'s top speed was 8 knots, or 9.2 miles per hour.

Tecumseh was armed with two XV-inch smoothbore Dahlgren guns mounted in a gun turret plated with ten inches of iron as well as the pilothouse. The XV-inch Dahlgren required ten minutes to load, aim and fire. With a weight of 45,000 pounds, they were the most powerful guns in the Union navy. "Early XV-inch Dahlgrens fired entirely within the turret, only the ball going through the gun port. This necessitated a 'smoke box' of iron plating around the muzzle to prevent the crew from being wiped out by the blast.

A major innovation of *Tecumseh* was the box was eliminated by widening the gun port, lengthening the gun 16 inches and turning it slim enough to enter the opening."[5]

The turret chamber contained two large-capacity (15,000 cubic feet per minute) blowers of the Dimpfels type. These blowers took air in through the top of the turret and discharged air through a branched duct system into the fire room, the officers' quarters and the berth deck.[6]

A ship's bell was located outside the turret during normal cruising operations but was moved inside the turret under combat conditions. Based on general ship plans of the period, communications from the pilothouse to the engine room were made through a speaking tube or voice pipe. Due to the engine room noise, a gong was mounted within the room to alert them when orders were about to be given. One of Commander Craven's real concerns was its buoyancy. Only a few hundred tons of water could sink the vessel.

Acknowledgements
and Preliminary Notes

L ike any project, research and people make it happen. I am deeply indebted to those who guided and supported me throughout the project. A special thanks to my good friend adjunct history professor Wayne Sirmon, who is not only a great historian but also a computer whiz. He encouraged me "not to give up the ship"; John Sledge, Mobile Historic Development Commission, for professional guidance; Heather Tassin and Dylan Tucker, Alabama Historical Commission, Fort Morgan Historic Site, for assistance with archival data; Paul Brueske, University of South Alabama; Stacey Hathorne, Alabama Historic Commission state archaeologist; Seth Conrad and Nick Beeson, History Museum of Mobile; Scotty Kirkland, State of Alabama Archives, Montgomery, AL; the Mobile Public Library, Local History Division; Shea McLean, curator, USS *Alabama* Memorial Park, Mobile; Dave Benway, Old Depot Museum, Vicksburg, MS; Allen Saltus, marine archaeologist, Jackson, LA; Jeffrey Seymour, director, National Civil War Naval Museum, Columbus, GA; Deborah Shapiro, archives technician, Smithsonian Institution, Washington, D.C., for photographs and vital information on participants in the 1967 excavations; M.C. Farrington, Hampton Roads Naval Museum, Norfolk, VA, for artifact photographs; Ms. Flint, Cornell University, Carl A. Kroch Library, Ithaca, NY; the New Jersey Maritime Museum, Beach Haven, NJ, Mary Ryan, curator; United States Naval Undersea Museum, Keyport, WA; Gordon B. Calhoun, historian/curator, Naval History and Heritage Command, Washington, D.C.; Wythe Whiting, Mobile, AL; Phillip Nassar, Mobile, AL; John Sellers, Mobile; Bob Holcombe, Columbus, GA; and Mike Bailey, Gulf Shores, AL.

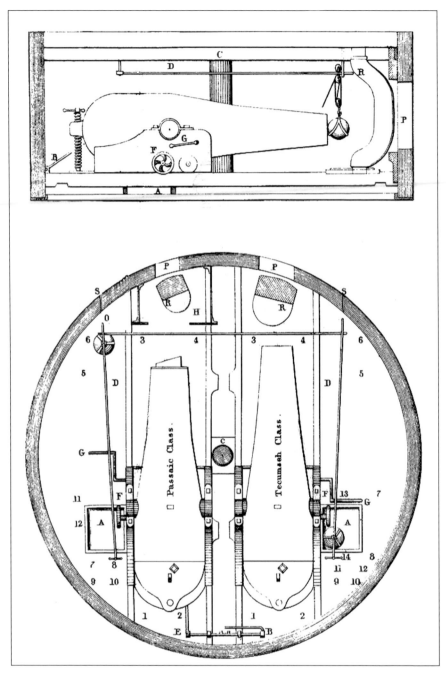

Two-gun turret with XV guns on the *Tecumseh*. *Warren Ripley, Artillery and Ammunition of the Civil War.*

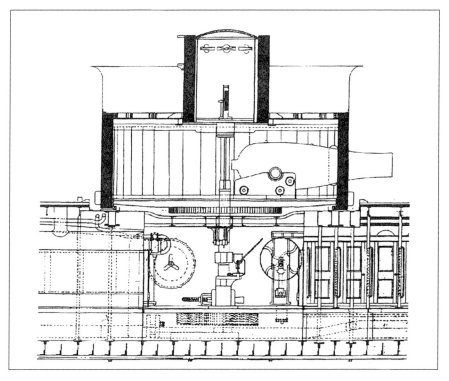

Turret and pilothouse of Passaic-class *Monitor* design by John Ericsson. *National Archives and Records Administration, Record Group 19, Ships Plan 1-10-28.*

Shot and shell were stored in magazines below the turret and hoisted by a set of blocks and beams that hung from the upper beams.

The powder charges in sacks, swabs and rammers around the shells were held by wrought iron hooks.[1]

Although the pilothouse was above the turret, it was stationary on a center shaft that did not turn with the turret.[2]

We will see in chapters 2 and 5 the result of men in combat facing the "fog of war." This uncertainty of awareness has plagued soldiers at war for centuries, as described by combatants on both sides of battle. There are several definitions of this term: the difficulty of making decisions in the midst of conflict; the uncertainty in situation awareness by participants in military operations; and the complexity of military conflicts.

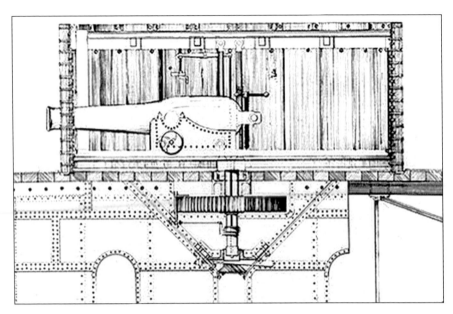

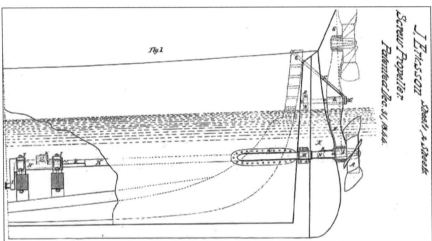

Top: Swedish engineer John Ericsson's gun turret design for the USS *Monitor*. *National Archives*.

Bottom: Screw propeller awarded to John Ericsson of New York, December 31, 1844. Design of the rudder and propeller for the USS *Monitor*. *Courtesy Hampton Roads Naval Museum © The Daybook. Patent number 3,689.*

Life aboard a Monitor-class ironclad was most unpleasant. The vessels were ugly, ungainly and remarkably unseaworthy. These ships were unlike any the world had ever seen, and living on one was so trying that the ordeal of battle was a welcomed relief. All hatches were battened down when at sea, causing the engine room to reach 130° Fahrenheit. Headaches and fainting spells were common. Monitors were dingy, hot, cramped, slow and hard to steer. They were leaky and wet. Monitors were designed for combat against other vessels, particularly ironclads.[3]

After 290 major changes in her construction, Tecumseh *was finally completed on March 17, 1864. After her commissioning on April 19th, she was placed under the command of Tunis Augustus Macdonough Craven and ordered to join the North Atlantic Blockading Fleet at Newport News, Virginia arriving on station on the 28th.*[4]

The image below is the only known photograph of *Tecumseh*, painted white, shortly after it was launched from the Jersey City, New Jersey shipyard in 1863.

USS *Tecumseh* at Jersey City Shipyard. *History Museum of Mobile, Alabama.*

1

TECUMSEH'S FIRST ASSIGNMENT

David Farragut planned to have *Tecumseh* lead the attack on Mobile Bay, but it was still in Hampton Roads. The trek from Hampton Roads to Mobile Bay would be long and ominous for Captain Tunis Craven and his crew. With the double-ended side-wheeler steamer *Eutaw* towing *Tecumseh* and side-wheeler *Augusta* as escort, it began the tumultuous trip to the Pensacola Navy Yard, now in Union hands, from Trent's Reach, Virginia, at 9:45 a.m. on July 5, 1864.

En route, its wheel ropes parted, causing the *Tecumseh* to run aground. The tiller ropes had burned in two by the heat of the boilers. With temporary repairs made, it sailed from Norfolk, arriving on July 8 at the naval station in Port Royal, South Carolina, where it remained for a week undergoing additional repairs. Farragut was becoming more anxious, as his target date for the attack, August 5, was drawing near, and there was no *Tecumseh* to lead his van of warships into battle. On July 28 at 7:00 a.m., *Tecumseh* was at anchor in Pensacola Bay opposite the navy yard. Once again, it was in great need of repairs. The trek from Norfolk to Pensacola had taken its toll on the crew, who were fatigued and sick from the trip. The following correspondence concerning the delay of *Tecumseh* took place between Farragut and his commanders on August 3 and August 4.

On June 19, 1864, off Cherbourg, France, the USS *Kearsarge* sank Raphael Semmes's CSS *Alabama*, prompting Farragut to write his son a letter on July 20: "The victory of the *Kearsarge* over the *Alabama* raised me up. I would sooner have fought that fight than any ever fought on the ocean."[1] Farragut was off of Mobile, preparing to attack, and thought it strange that very few from the Confederate side knew of that engagement.

Tecumseh at sea en route to Mobile Bay accompanied by USS *Augusta* (*right*) and USS *Eutaw* (*left*). Oil on canvas (1912), by Xanthus Smith, captain's clerk aboard USS *Augusta*. Dr. Charles V. Peery.

Tuesday, August 2, 1864

Captain Percival Drayton, USS Hartford *to Commander Thornton Jenkins, USS* Richmond:
"We are anxiously looking for you all, especially the Tecumseh. The Tecumseh must be got out when ready without being detained for anything."[2]

Captain Drayton to Commander Jenkins:
"Hurry up the Tecumseh, for the army will be ready to land on Wednesday on Dauphin Island."[3]

Rear Admiral Farragut to Lieutenant Commander Alexander Gibson, USS Potomac *at Pensacola:*
"If they are not here as soon as the Tecumseh, there will be no object in sending them, say to the commander of the Tecumseh that if he is ready on Wednesday afternoon and the weather is fine, he can come out without waiting for morning. Under no circumstances should Tecumseh be kept waiting for a tow."[4]

Rear Admiral Farragut to Lieutenant Henry Howison USS Bienville:
"Proceed at once to Pensacola with the Bienville and take the Tecumseh in tow as soon as she is ready and bring her out. She must be got off early tomorrow morning; otherwise she will be of no use to me in my operation."[5]

WEDNESDAY, AUGUST 3

Captain Drayton to Commander Jenkins:
"As the Tennessee has come out, we must have the Metacomet, Tecumseh or no Tecumseh."

Rear Admiral Farragut to Captain Jenkins:
"I have lost the finest day for my operations. I confidently supposed that the Tecumseh would be ready in four days and here we are on the sixth and no signs of her and I am told has just begin to coal. I could have done very well without her."[6]

THURSDAY, AUGUST 4

After topping off its coal bunkers with 150 tons of smokeless anthracite coal, *Tecumseh* left Pensacola about 10:00 a.m. on August 4, escorted by USS *Richmond*, and USS *Port Royal* and under tow of the USS *Bienville*, a converted civilian side-wheeler steamship. They made the fifty-five-mile trip in six hours, and no more was said concerning the delay.

Off of Mobile, on August 4, Farragut wrote the following letter to his wife in Hastings, New York:

> *My dearest wife, I write and leave this letter for you. I am going to Mobile Bay in the morning if "God is my leader" as I hope he is, and in him I place my trust, if he thinks it is the proper place for me to die I am ready to submit to his will, in that as all other things. My great mortification is that my vessels, the ironclads were not ready to have gone in yesterday. The army landed last night and are in full view of us this morning and the Tecumseh has not yet arrived from Pensacola. God bless and preserve you my darling and my dear boy, if anything should happen to me—and may his blessings also rest upon your dear mother and your sisters and their children.*
>
> *Your devoted and affectionate husband, who never for one moment forgot his love or fidelity to you his devoted and best of wives,*
>
> *Very truly yours*
> *D.G. Farragut*

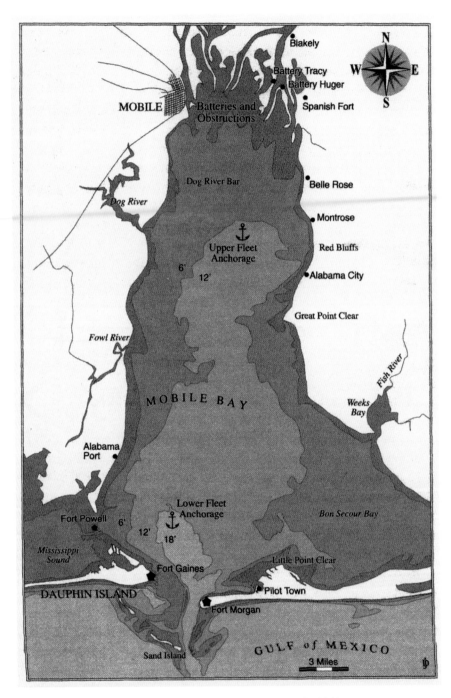

1864 map of the Mobile Bay showing battle area. *West Wind Flood Tide*.

FRIDAY, AUGUST 5

At half-past seven the Tecumseh was well up with the fort [Morgan], *having the Tennessee on the port beam. The monitor's guns had been loaded with steel shot and sixty pounds of powder, which at the time was the heaviest that had been attempted. Commander of the Tecumseh, Tunis A.M. Craven, knew that the eyes of all the fleet were upon him. It was his great opportunity to show his "trial of strength" against the formidable ram and Confederate Commander Franklin Buchanan.*[7]

The fire from the fort was scarcely noticed as the monitor steamed toward its adversary. As they drew near the buoy marking the easternmost limit of the torpedo field, Craven, from the pilothouse, saw it so close in line with the beach that he said to his pilot, "It is impossible that the admiral means for this vessel to go inside the buoy; I cannot turn the ship."[8]

2

TECUMSEH JOINS THE
GULF BLOCKADING SQUADRON

O n July 12, 1864, Farragut issued General Orders Number Ten to the fleet from aboard his flagship, USS *Hartford*, in preparation for the task at hand:

Strip your vessels and prepare for the conflict. Send down all your superfluous spars and rigging. Trice up or remove the whiskers. Put up the splinter nets on the starboard side and barricade the wheel and steersmen with sails and hammocks. Lay chains or sandbags on the deck over the machinery to resist a plunging fire. Hang the sheet chains over the side or make any other arrangement for security that your ingenuity may suggest. Land your starboard boats or lower and tow them on the port side and lower the port boats down to the water's edge. Place a leadsman and the pilot in the port quarter boat or the most convenient to the commander.

The vessels will run past the forts in couples lashed side by side as hereafter designated. The flag ship will lead and steer from Sand Island N. by E. by compass until abreast of Fort Morgan, then N.W. half N. until past the middle ground, then N. by W. and the others, as designated in the drawing, will follow in due order until ordered to anchor, but the bow and quarter line must be preserved to give the chase guns a fair range and each vessel must be kept astern of the broadside of the next ahead; each vessel will keep a very little on the starboard quarter of his next ahead and when abreast of the fort will keep directly astern and as we pass the fort, will take the same distance on the port quarter of the next ahead to enable the stern guns to fire clear of the next vessel astern.

It will be the object of the admiral to get as close to the fort as possible before opening fire. The ships, however, will open fire the moment the enemy opens upon us with their chase and other guns as fast as they can be brought to bear. Use short fuses for the shell and shrapnel, and as soon as within 300 or 400 yards, give them grape. It is understood that heretofore we have fired too high, but with grapeshot it is necessary to elevate a little above the object, as grape will dribble from the muzzle of the gun.

If one or more of the vessels be disabled, their partners must carry them through, if possible, but if they cannot then the next astern must render the required assistance, but as the admiral contemplates moving with the flood tide, it will only require sufficient power to keep the crippled vessels in the channel.

Vessels that can must place guns upon the poop and topgallant forecastle and in the tops on the starboard side. Should the enemy fire grape, they will remove the men from the topgallant forecastle and poop guns below until out of grape range.

The howitzers must keep up a constant fire from the time they can reach with shrapnel until out of its range.[1]

On Friday, August 5, 1864, at 6:00 a.m., Farragut's van of four monitors and fourteen wooden warships proceeded on their mission to destroy Forts Morgan, Gaines and Powell and the Confederate fleet. Standing on the southwest bastion of Fort Morgan, Confederate artillery Captain Wythe Whiting knew what was going on: the enemy was preparing to attack just before daylight.

With the monitors *Tecumseh* and *Manhattan* each carrying two XV-inch guns, the *Winnebago* and *Chickasaw* each carrying four XI-inch guns in single file leading the fourteen that were lashed together two by two, they began their advance. The fleet consisted of the following vessels and their number of guns in order: *Brooklyn* (twenty-six), *Octorara* (ten), *Hartford* (twenty-eight), *Metacomet* (ten), *Richmond* (twenty four), *Port Royal* (eight), *Lackawanna* (fourteen), *Seminole* (nine), *Monongahela* (twelve), *Kennebec* (five), *Ossipee* (thirteen), *Itasca* (four), *Oneida* (ten) and *Galena* (fourteen). It took thirty minutes for the fleet to fully engage the fort. Then, at 6:30 a.m., *Tecumseh* fired the first volley with 440-pound shells. From his vantage point at the fort's water battery, Captain Whiting witnessed the shell hitting the base of the brick lighthouse on Mobile Point.[2]

Fort Morgan's guns had little effect on the low profile of the monitors. The turret held twenty men plus two officers within its twenty-foot diameter and included the two XV-inch Dahlgerns. From this position, a gunner spotted a red buoy off the port side that marked the vast field of submerged torpedoes. The pilot exclaimed, "I cannot turn the ship!" Just before ramming the CSS *Tennessee* at the head of the field, *Tecumseh* struck a torpedo. It immediately lurched from side to side, careened violently over and went down bow first, its propeller still turning in the air. In less than two minutes, it was on the bottom, upside down at 155 degrees. Confederate fleet surgeon D.B. Conrad was aboard the *Tennessee*: "We observed one of the monitors was apparently at a standstill; she lay to for a moment, seemed to reel, then slowly disappear into the gulf. Immediately immense bubbles of steam as large as cauldrons rose to the surface of the water and only eight human beings could be seen in the turmoil." Confederate forces ceased firing during rescue operations.

The monitor's sudden loss caused USS *Brooklyn*, stationed immediately ahead of Farragut's flagship USS *Hartford*, to begin to falter. Farragut knew the other warships could not continue forward. Ships of that time were equipped with a speaking tube and signal flags, enabling commands to be given to the deck officer, who passed commands to the helmsman. A bell-pull officer communicated with the engine room by a series of strokes. One

USS *Tecumseh* going down after hitting torpedo. *Smithsonian Institution, SIA 2020-002845.*

Admiral David Glasgow Farragut in the rigging of his flagship, USS *Hartford*. The *Tecumseh* is in the foreground. *Smithsonian Institution, SIA 2020-002846.*

pull meant "go ahead"; two pulls meant "stop"; three, "back"; four, "go ahead full speed." Tom Williamson, *Hartford*'s chief engineer, heard Farragut order "go ahead." Williamson asked, "Shall I ring four bells sir?" Farragut replied, "Four bells, eight bells, sixteen bells, damn it, I don't care how many bells you ring."[3]

THE RESCUE

Aboard the *Tecumseh*, "the pilot leaped from the pilot house and half a dozen sailors in the turret managed to jump through the ports. Farragut, from his post in the port main-rigging, hailed [Lieutenant Commander James E.] Jouett, who was standing on top of the pilothouse of the *Metacomet*, to know if he had a boat that he could send to pick up the survivors. Jouett had anticipated the order, and a boat in charge of Ensign H.C. Neilds, a volunteer officer, was about leaving the port quarter of the gunboat."[4]

From a crew of 114 Union sailors aboard *Tecumseh*, there were 21 survivors. Seven survived by one of the lifeboats located on deck just behind the pilothouse: Acting Master C.F. Langley (officer), Acting Master Gordon Cottrell (officer), Gunner's Mate S.S. Shinn, Quarter Gunner John Gould, Seaman Frank Commens, Seaman Richard Collins and Seaman Peter Parker.

Ten men were rescued by USS *Metacomet*, commanded by Acting Ensign Henry C. Neilds: Acting Ensign John P. Zettick (officer), Quartermaster Chauncy Dean, Quartermaster William Roberts, Seaman James McDonald, Seaman George Major, Seaman James Thorn, Ordinary Seaman Charles Packard, Landsman William Fetter, Coal Heaver William C. West and Civilian Pilot John Collins.

Four sailors swam to shore at Fort Morgan, were captured at the guardhouse and sent to Andersonville Prison in Americus, Georgia: George C. Overton, J. Loughray, P. McGinnis and a Mr. Ferrell.[5]

Several years after the war, an interview was held aboard the *Frolic* in Gibraltar Harbor by Rear Admiral Casper A. Goodrich, U.S. Navy, with Acting Master Gardner Cottrell, a survivor of the *Tecumseh*, to reflect on that infamous day in August 1864.

> *I wonder if any of you can forget his sensations on the eve of battle. Today has been exactly like that preceding the fight: something in the air has brought it all back to me and I have been living over and over the experiences of that thrilling event. The extraordinary nature of one of its happenings I have never understood for it borders on miraculous....*
>
> *Has it ever occurred to any of you, asked Dr. Bank* [Dr. Henry A. Danker was the ship's surgeon] *that there may be torpedoes planted in the channel and that the Tecumseh is no better if she is not indeed rather worse than a wooden vessel in the event of running upon them.*
>
> *I was fortunate enough to be on the birth deck just under the turret, at my station in the powder division, when the shock came and the sea began to pour in. I shouted to the few men near me to climb up through the turret, and joining them, all of us hurried to keep ahead of the water. We crawled through the 15-inch gun port and among the last, I reached the deck as the ship gave a lurch and settled heavy. Running to the side I jumped overboard and struck out as hard as I could, fearing to be sucked down with the Tecumseh which I realized was hopelessly lost....*

Acting master of USS *Tecumseh*, Gardner Cottrell, one of the survivors swimming away from the undertow of the sinking vessel. Deseret Evening News, *August 29, 1910.*

It seemed as an eternity before I came up to the top again. I was nearly exhausted but I struggled to regain my breath…when a heavy wave came along from I don't know where, and swamped me entirely….Once more I saw the light of day, filled my lungs with fresh air and managed to keep afloat by treading water….I was picked up by one of our boats [off *Tecumseh*].[6]

Flag ship Hartford, W.G. Blockading Squadron
Mobile Bay, August 27, 1864

SIR, I have the honor to forward herewith (marked No. 1) a copy of a report made to me by Acting Masters C.F. Langley and Gardner Cottrell, two of the survivors of the iron-clad Tecumseh, and in which are given the names of six men who were saved in the same boat. These officers are certainly in error in their statement that a row of buoys stretched from the shore a distance of one to two hundred yards. We know that the channel adjacent to the shore was entirely clear of torpedoes, and that the latter were placed between large buoys, to which I have referred in my report.[7]

Very Respectfully, your obedient servant,
D.G. Farragut
Rear Admiral, Commanding W.G.B. Squadron.

The Saturday, August 13, 1864 edition of the *New York Times* reported two firsthand accounts:

THE DEPARTMENT OF THE GULF:
OUR VICTORY BELOW MOBILE
A DISPATCH FROM GEN. BANKS
A MONITOR SUNK BY TORPEDO

The steamer Evening Star from New Orleans August 6th arrived at this port yesterday. By her we received a brief but satisfactory confirmation of the great success achieved at Mobile by Admiral Farragut. It comes in the shape of a telegram from Gen. Banks to Mrs. Banks who was a passenger on the Evening Star. The dispatch was put on board the Evening Star as she was passing the station at quarantine below New Orleans.

OFFICE OF THE MILITARY TELEGRAPH
New Orleans, Saturday, Aug 6th.[8]

FORT PIKE, NEW ORLEANS AUGUST 6th.

Steamer Clyde passed here this morning from the fleet. She reports that fourteen gunboats and three monitors past the forts at Mobile yesterday at 8 a.m. One monitor was blown up opposite the forts by a torpedo. The rebel ram Tennessee was captured. Her Captain, Buchanan lost a leg in the fight.

This gives us possession.
I have no other particulars.
N.P. Banks
Major-Gen. Commanding[9]

The weak fortifications at Mobile, and the mere pretense of a naval flotilla that the Confederate government had been able to provide for the defense of the city, had proved wholly insufficient to resist the vigorous attack of Admiral Farragut's powerful fleet.[10]

3

TORPEDOES

One of the major points of debate among Confederate leaders during the Civil War was the use of torpedoes or mines against Northern military naval sources, merchants and civilians. President Jefferson Davis, who thought they were unethical and cowardly weapons, was opposed to using them in almost every context. Many of his advisors felt otherwise, and as the Confederate war effort grew direr in 1864, their calls became louder. "The torpedoes were the most striking and effective of the new contrivance for defense which were used during these operations. Every avenue to approach to the outworks or to the City of Mobile was guarded by submarine torpedoes."[1] Davis's opposition to torpedoes does not mean they were not used; indeed, since the war began, Missouri Confederates, acting undercover along St. Louis piers, had been sabotaging Union shipping on the Mississippi and Missouri Rivers by placing explosives in the firewood used for fuel on steamboats. Throughout the war, torpedo makers there and elsewhere in the South were honing their craft and looking for new ways to disguise their explosives, and they were spurred on by a new Confederate law passed in a secret congressional session authorizing rewards for inventors of new technologies, including submersibles and mines. The Confederate States was the first government to bring torpedoes into warfare as a legitimate weapon. Three of the most prolific inventors of the torpedo were Gabriel J. Rains, E.C. Singer and J.R. Fretwell.

On October 31, 1862, the Congress of the Confederate States of America passed a bill authorizing two new divisions of the Navy Department. Brigadier General Gabriel J. Rains was placed in charge of the Torpedo Bureau, and under the direction of Matthew Fontaine Maury, Lieutenant Hunter Davidson was named to command the Naval Submarine Battery Service. The purpose of both bureaus was to investigate, organize and improve creative methods of "torpedo" warfare, what would today be described as mines.

Their deadly inventions were placed in Mobile Bay in anticipation of Farragut's navy attacking Mobile in 1862, right after the fall of New Orleans. General Banks, however, ordered Farragut to the Red River campaign to cut off the lower forts on the lower Mississippi River and Vicksburg. As a result of the torpedoes having been in place for two years before the Union navy moved on Mobile, the majority of the torpedoes had become waterlogged, and the powder was ineffective. Before the battle, Farragut sent out crews in small boats by night to attempt to clear the channel. The Confederate Torpedo Service had laid out 180 torpedoes in three rows, leaving a small gap in the channel to permit blockade runners access to the upper bay. As the Union fleet waited for *Tecumseh* to join it from Pensacola, four reconnaissance trips into Mobile Bay failed to locate the torpedo field that deserters had reported.

Minesweeping operations by Union navy attempting to clear torpedoes from the bay. *USS Tecumseh Shipwreck Management Plan.*

The sinking of *Tecumseh* was "the most completely disabling blow struck by torpedoes during the entire war."[2] "The Federal attack would not have been succeeded!—nay—it would even have resulted in disaster to Admiral Farragut's fleet—had it been possible to obstruct the channel between Fort Morgan and the eastern bank. All the Confederates had to do was place torpedoes across the western portion of the channel. The Federals knew about the gap." "In addition to *Tecumseh*, eleven other Federal vessels, including warships and transports, were sunk in Mobile Bay and Blakeley River by torpedoes."[3]

Here is an example of misinformation communicated by Major General Dabney H. Maury to headquarters fifty-two days after the battle:

HEADQUARTERS DISTRICT OF THE GULF,
Mobile, Ala., September 26, 1864

I ordered a space on the line of torpedoes to be left open for the Tennessee and other ships to pass in and out. This space was marked by a buoy 160 yards from the Fort Morgan shore. A ship passing between that buoy and the shore would be exposed to the fire at short range of seven 10-inch Columbaids, three 8-inch guns, two 8-inch Blakely rifles, two 7-inch Brooke rifles, some six 4.1-inch rifles, several 32-pounders, and the rifle fire of the sharpshooters. No vessel yet built could pass through the channel in daylight. The enemy gave it a wide berth on the 5th August. From the best information I can procure, none of their ships passed within 800 yards of Fort Morgan. All of them passed over the torpedoes. The Tecumseh is believed by General Page to have been sunk by his fire. She is claimed by some to have been sunk by a Singer torpedo; by Lieutenant Barrett, in his paper, to have been sunk by one of General Rains' torpedoes. It is probable that the rapid and changing currents in the deep channel off Morgan, and other causes operating there, had carried away many of the torpedoes and injured others. Captain Bennett, of Fort Gaines, thinks the Tecumseh sunk 400 to 500 yards from shore; that the rest of the fleet passed 500 or 600 yards from shore. Major St. Paul says they passed so far from shore that the howitzers in the tops of the ships failed to reach the shore with their projectiles.[4]
Respectfully, &c.

Dabney H. Maury,
Major General, Commanding

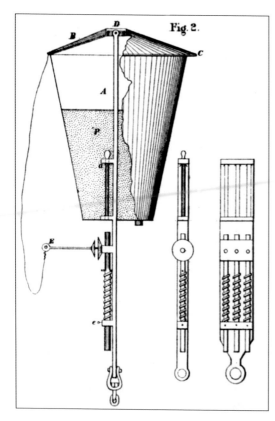

Left: Confederate torpedo experts J.R. Fretwell and E.C. Singer designed, built and laid three rows of mines from Fort Morgan to Fort Gaines in an effort to keep the bay clear of Union ships. *National Archives*.

Below: Gabriel J. Rains invented and built the keg torpedo design. Harper's Weekly, *April 29, 1865*.

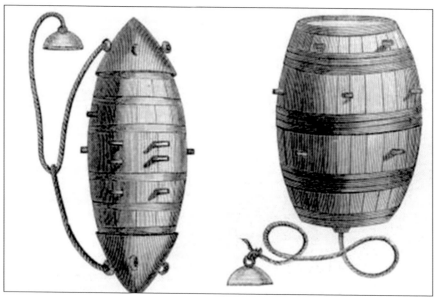

Mobile Bay and the Blakeley River, on the eastern shore of adjoining Baldwin County, saw the most deadly torpedo sinkings of the war:

August 5, 1865	Mobile Bay	USS *Tecumseh*, monitor	Sunk
December 7, 1864	Mobile Bay	*Narcissus*, tug	Sunk
March 12, 1865	Blakeley River	*Althea*, gunboat	Sunk
March 28, 1865	Blakeley River	USS *Milwaukee*, monitor	Sunk
March 29, 1865	Blakeley River	USS *Osage*, monitor	Sunk
April 1, 1865	Blakeley River	USS *Randolph*, gunboat	Sunk
April 13, 1865	Blakeley River	*Ida*, tug	Sunk
April 14, 1865	Mobile Bay	USS *Scotia*, gunboat	Sunk
April 14, 1865	Blakeley River	*Cincinnati's* launch	Sunk
May 12, 1865	Mobile Bay	*R.B. Hamilton*, transport	Sunk[5]

Ironclads are not to master the world, but torpedoes master the ironclads.[6]

While obstructions were being cleared on November 10, 1864, the 420-pound, class-9 Rebel frame torpedo (seen in the image below) used to protect obstructions in the Mobile River just north of the city was recovered.

Dismounted Confederate frame torpedo. *U.S. Naval Undersea Museum, Keyport, Washington.*

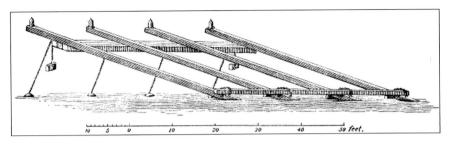

Mounted Confederate frame torpedo. *Victor Von Sheliha, Treatise on Coast Defense.*

"Live shells were mounted to timbers attached to wooden frames or cribs that were anchored in rows to the bottom of the waterway with heavy stones.

"These were placed just beneath the surface in harbors, rivers and bays. When a ship passed over them, the contact pressure crushed the torpedoes' copper cap and ignited its fuse."[7]

Frame torpedoes were one of the most successful types of torpedo used by the Confederacy. "Inventors like David Bushnell, Robert Fulton and Samuel Colt had experimented with underwater mines (torpedoes) leading up to the war, laying the groundwork for future innovations."[8]

4

THE FORTS

I n 1812, the United States Congress recognized the necessity for defense of Mobile Bay. In 1819, it authorized two forts to be built at the mouth of the bay. Today, Fort Morgan at Mobile Point in Baldwin County and, three miles to the west, Fort Gaines on Dauphin Island, were the result of that action. The remnant of Fort Powell, a smaller fortification at Grant's Pass on Mississippi Sound, was also engaged in defense. To the west, the city of Mobile was protected by more than forty forts and redoubts in concentric circles. As a result, Mobile was considered the most fortified city in the South.

The American system of fort building was greatly influenced by the French school of military architecture. These forts were initially designed in an age of deep-draft, wind-driven wooden sailing ships. Both the North and the South depended on these brick-and-mortar forts to stave off seaward attacks. The Civil War was the first modern war that produced ironclad- and monitor-type warships and rifled guns. The impact of shells on brick and mortar crumbled the masonry walls.

Renowned Prussian engineer Viktor Von Scheliha worked for the Confederacy to shore up the fortifications in Mobile by modifying coastal defense works. The most significant development was the introduction of large mounds of sand piled inside the walls of the forts to absorb the heavy impact of exploding shells and to prevent the outer perimeter walls from being penetrated. In some places, sod was planted and sandbags filled by Mobile schoolgirls held the sand in place. "No ship or floating battery, however heavily she may be plated, can cope successfully with a *properly* constructed fortification of masonry. The one is fixed and immovable and though constructed of material which may be shattered by shot, can be covered if need be, by the same or much heavier armor than floating vessels can bear. The other is subject to disturbances by winds and waves, and to the powerful effects of tides and currents."[1]

On a map published in 1863 by G.W. Tomlinson of Boston is listed a chart of armament within all the fortifications of the Mobile Bay defenses.

Type	Guns
Forty-two-pounders	14
Twenty-four-pounders	52
Eighteen-pounders	3
Twelve-pounders	4
Brass field pieces	6
Brass-flanking howitzers	26
Eight-inch howitzers, heavy	10
Thirteen-inch mortars	2
Ten-inch mortars, heavy	4
Ten-inch mortars, light	2
Sixteen-inch stone mortars	2
Eight-inch mortars, light	2
Coehorn mortars	6
Total Armament	133

It is believed that all or nearly all of the guns required for this armament of the work were within its walls. The fort has simple quarters for officers and soldiers, barracks, storehouses and magazines and furnaces for heating hot shot. The entire work cost $1.25 million.

FORT MORGAN

From these walls, Confederate gunners fired on the Federal fleet at close range, as the obstructions in the channel forced the fleet to pass close under the guns of the fort. The fort fired over 490 shots, an average of 8 shots a minute, while the vessels were in range. The five-sided fort mounted its guns in three tiers, and when the fighting was at its peak, the firing became even more rapid.

1864 Fort Morgan interior battle damage. *Fort Morgan Museum.*

1864 Fort Morgan south wall battle damage. *Fort Morgan Museum.*

The Hot Shot Furnace at Fort Morgan

Another weapon used against an attack by wooden warships was developed in antiquity by the Britons to burn Roman encampments. It has been referred to as "Greek fire," because heated clay balls were used as projectiles. Catapults hurled the fireballs into besieged castles and towns in the classical and medieval periods.

With the development of the cannon and the use of gunpowder, projectiles were modified to cause fires.

> *The use of heated projectiles became increasingly important over the next two hundred years, especially against ships. During the American Revolutionary War, American and French artillerymen burned the 44-gun British warship HMS Charon with hot shot during the Battle of Yorktown in 1781. Perhaps the most famous use of hot-shot took place in 1782 during the second siege of Gibraltar when French and Spanish forces attempted to use ten large floating batteries in a bombardment against British defenders. The floating batteries had been made of heavy construction and were thought to be invincible. However, British artillery in Gibraltar used hot shot to destroy nine of the ten batteries and inflict a loss of 1500 crewmen.*[2]

Totten hot shot furnace at Fort Morgan. The furnace was used to heat solid-shot cannon balls fired at the rigging and wooden decks of attacking ships. *Courtesy National Park Service.*

The same hot shot furnace completely restored. *Courtesy Fort Morgan Historical Site.*

In 1816, French engineer General Simon Bernard, the head of the board of fortifications, came to the United States with the idea of hot shot furnaces to defend the coastal fortifications. The furnaces were constructed of various sizes depending on the number of shot they would hold. At one end is the firebox; the chimney is at the opposite end. Sloping iron rails held the cannonballs, and the oven's interior was fire brick. Solid-shot cannonballs were placed on the iron rails and rolled down to the firebox. The iron stars on the outside of the furnace were used to hold up the iron rails inside. The larger furnaces could hold as many as sixty cannonballs.

It took a three-man crew to operate the furnace: one to maintain the fire and add the cold cannonballs; one to remove the heated cannonballs; and one to clean them. The furnace at Fort Morgan received most of its damage through neglect but has been restored to its original condition.

Fort Morgan's artillery consisted of seven 10.0-inch Columbaids, three 8.0-inch Columbaids and twenty-two 32-pounder smoothbores, two 6.5-inch and four 5.8-inch. The water battery mounted 10-inch Columbaids, an 8.0-inch and two 32-pounders.[3]

Fort Powell

Commanded by Lieutenant Colonel James W. Williams of the Twenty-First Alabama Infantry Volunteers of Mobile, Fort Powell was constructed north of Grant's Pass and protected it in the best manner possible under the circumstances. Sand batteries were erected on either side of the little island on which the keeper of the pass and light used to live.

From February 16 until March 2, 1864, Farragut bombarded the fort with his fleet of mortar boats, *Port Royal, Calhoun, Sea Foam, Chickasaw* and *Sarah Bruen*, and warships *J.P. Jackson, Octorara, John Griffith, Henry James, O.H. Lee* and *Sebago*. Due to the very shallow water, the closest the fleet could get was eight hundred yards.

With tons of shells fired at Fort Powell, not a single gun was dismounted, not a single traverse was seriously damaged, nor were the parapet or bombproof. The parapet—a wall built of earth, sand or rocks to protect the soldiers—was eight feet high and twenty-five feet thick. On each face of the work, three guns were mounted, each with its own chamber eighteen feet in diameter. The bombproof contained the powder magazine, a shell-filling room, laboratory, blacksmith shop, water tank, surgeon's room and quarters for the men. A covered passageway established safe communications between the gun pits, and each gun had its own service magazine. The fort was armed with three 7.0-inch Brooke rifles, one 6.4-inch Columbaid, one 8.0-inch Columbaid, one 10.0-inch Columbaid and one 32-pounder.

Fort Gaines

Commanded by General Charles Anderson of the Twenty-First Alabama Regiment, the pentagon-shaped Fort Gaines is a typical brick-and-mortar fortification named for General Edmund Pendleton Gaines, who led the capture of Vice President Aaron Burr in Washington County, Alabama, in February 1807.

On the easternmost point of Dauphin Island is a fortified defense fort with twenty-two-foot-high walls surrounded by a dry moat thirty-five feet wide. Bastions with connecting tunnels and wide brick gun ramps for ammunition carts led to the gun platforms, where twenty-six mounted guns were placed in a barbette on top of the fort walls. The largest gun was a ten-inch Columbaid. Surrounding the parade field were five buildings containing barracks for

Fort Gaines on the western end of Dauphin Island, three and a half miles west of Fort Morgan. *Fort Gaines Historic Site.*

the four hundred garrisoned members of the Alabama Militia, a kitchen, a dining hall, a laundry and a blacksmith shop, among other facilities. The fort was designed to survive a six-month siege.

Between August 3 and 8, 1864, Union major general Gordon Granger landed 1,500 troops seven miles west of the fort and began his siege. Unfortunately for the Confederates, Fort Gaines had little effect on Farragut's fleet three miles to the east.

> *Dauphin Island*
> *August 5, 1864*
> [General E.R.S. Canby:]
>
> *MY DEAR GENERAL: Yesterday was a glorious day for our cause. The Admiral, with his usual good luck and pluck, succeeded beyond all expectations, and in spite of all Fort Morgan and the rebel fleet could do.*
>
> *The firing was perhaps the heaviest and fiercest of anything on record. The game little monitor [Tecumseh] which led the fleet went down almost like a flash just inside the light-house, supposed to have run into a torpedo or other obstruction.*
>
> *Fort Gaines is closely invested; our pickets in are half a mile of the glacis and the line of battle one mile. Engineer Captains [Miles D.] McAlester and [John C.] Palfrey coincides with me in the opinion*

that [it] *is neither practicable nor profitable to besiege Gaines, but that Morgan is the first objective point, and that its early investment is of vital importance to the fleet.*[4]

Yours Truly,

G. GRANGER

HDQRS. Military Division of West Mississippi

New Orleans, La., August 6, 1864.

Maj. Gen. W.T. Sherman:

The fleet under Admiral Farragut passed the forts at the entrance of Mobile Bay at 8:00 o'clock yesterday morning. The monitor Tecumseh was blown up by a rebel torpedo and lost, with nearly all her crew. The rebel-ram Tennessee and gunboat Selma were captured after an obstinate resistance. The other gunboats took shelter under the guns of Fort Morgan. The admiral expects to capture or destroy them today, and to secure a landing east of Fort Morgan and in the bay for our troops. Fort Powell is reported abandoned and blown up. Fort Gaines was invested by the land forces of General Granger, and is reported to have surrendered, but this is not official. The loss in the fleet in killed, wounded and drowned is about 250. With the exception of the Tecumseh, none of the vessels were lost and the Hartford is the only one that is seriously injured.[5]

Ed. R.S. Canby,

Major-General

5

PERSONAL OBSERVATIONS

The Fog of War

I t is a known fact that eyewitnesses often recall the same instances in different detail. This was especially true during the sinking of *Tecumseh* on August 5, 1864. Although many witnessed the event, most witnesses observed from different perspectives.

Captain Julian Wythe (J.W.) Whiting,
First Alabama Battalion of Artillery

At 6:47 a.m., Captain Julian Whiting, commanding the water battery, observed a puff of white smoke from the *Tecumseh* and then, in seconds, a bright flash and loud explosion of the 350-pound shell as it smashed into the base of Mobile Point Lighthouse, sending brick and mortar everywhere.

Standing next to Whiting, General Page ordered Whiting to "open the fight." "The battery also fired on a small gunboat that attempted to pass the fort and sank it, leaving two or three dead upon her deck. Fort Morgan caught fire and the inside of the fort was like a furnace. In order to prevent an explosion to the magazines, all the powder had to be moved and poured into cisterns. Had the magazines exploded, the fort and all in it would have blown into the gulf. On August 23rd the white flag went up."[1]

Captain Whiting was taken prisoner and taken to New Orleans. "We reached New Orleans just before nightfall and were marched along the main street to prison. On Sunday morning at one o'clock I had escaped from prison. Before day break, I had found a friendly house." There were six others who also escaped. Whiting made his way to Natchez, changed his name to Francis Delano and returned to Mobile, where he resumed his duties to the Confederacy.

Fort Whiting Alabama National Guard Armory at 6120 South Broad Street in Mobile is named in his honor.

Confederate Second Lieutenant Huricosco Austill, Fort Morgan, August 1864

Appointed second lieutenant of the First Alabama Battery of Artillery, Austill was stationed at the water battery on the outer defenses of the southernmost point of Fort Morgan. His observations were recorded in his journal, which had been concealed in a thick comforter that his mother had made for him.

With the blockade of southern ports by Union warships laying six miles out from the entrance to Mobile Bay for the last three years, very little activity occurred except for an occasional blockade runner entering the bay under the cloak of darkness. In June of 1864, the ironclad ram Tennessee crossed Dog River bar into the bay with the intention of engaging the blockading fleet but soon thought better of it. In the third week of July, an ocean steamer towing a single turret monitor approached from the east. At once the garrison at Fort Morgan began to prepare for an attack from the Union fleet. Four days later, two double turret monitors came from the west through Mississippi Sound from New Orleans to join her.[2]

John C. O'Connell, C.S. Navy, Second Assistant Engineer CSS *Tennessee*

On July 22, one ironclad monitor arrived in the Yankee fleet which produced a great deal of excitement on board on account of her heading up the main channel. We immediately had decks cleared for action. She stopped and came to anchor. About the 28th another ironclad arrived off this port and the 29th another arrived. On the morning of the fifth, there was quite a commotion in the Yankee fleet. At about six o'clock the enemy fleet was discovered to be under way heading in towards Fort Morgan in the main channel. We discovered that the fleet was reinforced by another ironclad monitor [Tecumseh] coming in. The monitor which was in the lead was destroyed by a torpedo. There were only fifteen or twenty men saved including only two officers, the pilot and ensign.[3]

Sergeant Robert B. Tarpley, CS Army, First Tennessee Heavy Artillery

[August 6]

Since last writeing [sic] the Enemy has been reinforced by three ironclads. One of the ironclads opened on Fort Gains [sic] yesterday she done no damage. This morning at six o'clock two monitors, two ironclads and twelve sloops of war advanced steadily on the fort (Morgan). The long roll was beat and all went to their guns amidiately [sic].[4]

Landsman Ebson C. Lambert, U.S. Navy, Aboard USS *Itasca*

"We all have laurels on our brows about a foot deep." On August 5, 1864, I was instructed to get everything ready for the battle, distribute tourniquets to the officers and men. At 3 a.m. we hove up anchor and ran.

Along side the USS Ossipee and all ships fell in line, 14 in numbers. The ironclads took the lead and at 8:16 a.m. we had passed the forts. Early in the battle we had witnessed the sinking of the USS Tecumseh by a torpedo with all hands on board.[5]

First Lieutenant Joseph Biddle Wilkinson, First Tennessee Heavy Artillery, Fort Morgan

August 5, heavy musket fire at Fort Gaines about 5 am. On getting up at 6 a.m., saw Hartford and Brooklyn on right of the fleet; thought something was up. Walked down to the fort, by the time I reached the parapet the whole fleet were under way and steaming slowly upon the following order; single turreted monitors in advance, double turreted next, then the Hartford and Brooklyn with double-enders lashed to their port sides, the three masters and their gunboats lashed two and two following.

We opened on the flagship about a mile. The enemy did not open fire till within three quarters when broadside after broadside shook the very earth though apparently that was the only trembling for our men stood nobly to their guns. The action grows more terrific and the fleet is within two hundred yards of our batteries and abreast of the fort. The foremost ironclad Tecumseh sinks to rise no more and a tomb for one hundred and six corpses.[6]

Dr. William F. Hutchison, Assistant Surgeon, Aboard USS *Lackawanna*

Captain Craven was partly already out of the pilot house, when pilot, John Collins grasped him by the leg and cried, "let me get out first, Captain, for God's sake; I have five little children!" The Captain drew back, saying "go on sir," gave him his place and went down with his ship, while the pilot was saved.

The escape hatch, near the pilothouse, was the Achilles heel of the monitors, wide enough to allow only a single man out at a time. The turret of the Tecumseh was a sealed tomb, although two or three gunners squeezed through the narrow ports.[7]

Captain Percival Drayton Aboard the *Hartford*

On August 5, 1864, Captain Drayton wrote: "About 7:35 I heard the cry that a monitor was sinking, and looking on the starboard bow saw the turret of the *Tecumseh* just disappearing under the water, where in an instant before I had seen this noble vessel pushing on gallantly in a straight line to attack the enemy's ram *Tennessee*, which apparently moved out to give her an opportunity."[8]

On November 9, 1864, Admiral Farragut sent a note to Secretary of the Navy Gideon Welles: "Sir: I have had an application from an officer of this squadron—who was formally connected with a Boston firm of which Mr. T.H. Bacon is the principle partner. The firm is anxious to undertake to raise the *Tecumseh* and I understand their terms to be that the Government shall pay the sum or sums which may be agreed upon when the work is done. Much valuable material and her guns may be recovered, provided good divers are employed on this duty. There are none to be had here.

Those which I had at work on the *Phillipi* [*sic*] and the blockade runner *Ivanhoe* were good for nothing."[9]

The *Philippi* was initially the Confederate ship CSS *Ella* but was captured on November 10, 1863, and placed into service with the U.S. Navy as USS *Philippi* on February 23, 1864. It served as a patrol and picket boat in Mobile Bay until it was destroyed by Confederate guns while following Farragut on August 5, 1864.

Secretary Wells replied on November 15, 1864, "SIR: The relatives of the officers who were lost in the *Tecumseh* have been writing to the Department with regard to the possibility of raising the vessel or recovering the bodies or the personal effects of those who went down with her."[10]

Unfortunately, no attempt was made by the navy.

Private Charles Brother, USMC, Aboard USS *Hartford*

Charles Brother wrote on Friday, August 5, 1864, "All hands called out at 3 o'clock. At 5:30 the *Metacomet* came alongside and made fast to us. Other vessels of the fleet paired off in the same manner. Got under way about 6:30 and steamed toward Fort Morgan. The *Brooklyn* taking the lead, we, following her and the *Richmond* next after us. The fort opened fire at us about ten minutes past seven, just after we commenced firing, following the monitors. The *Tecumseh* sunk. She had her bottom blown out by a torpedo and went down like a shot."[11]

Captain James Alden's Logbook via Lieutenant Thomas L. Swann, USS *Brooklyn*'s Sailing Master

At 3 a.m. called all hands. At 5 the Octorara came along side. Lashed her to out port side. At 5:15 called all hands up the line; the monitors standing out from Sand Island. At 5:40 beat to quarters general action. Made every preparation for meeting the enemy. At 6 heading up the channel, followed by the rest of the fleet, the Hartford directly astern of us and the ironclads off our starboard bow. At 6:50 first shot fired by the enemy at this ship; immediately replied to by our bow chaser, a 100 pounder-Parrott, which commenced the engagement. At 7:20 fairly abreast of fort [Morgan] under a sharp fire. Rebel ram Tennessee with her gunboats, opened fire on us. Cast off the Octorara. The fort and batteries well silenced.

At 7:25 ironclad Tecumseh was sunk almost instantaneously by a torpedo. Rebel ram making for us. Backed the ship clear of two buoys, evidently attached to torpedoes.[12]

Captain J.B. Marchand, Steam Log, USS *Lackawanna*, Log via First Assistant Engineer

From midnight to 4 a.m., fires banked; distilling apparatus in operation during the watch. From 4 a.m. to 12 meridian: fires banked; 5:44, commenced spreading fires and working the engines per bell. There is a great deal of stopping, moving ahead and backing from 5:55 a.m. to 7:23 due to the uneven flow of the Union ships passing the fort. The Lackawanna fired its first shot at Fort Morgan at 7:30. Passed the fort at 8:11 to engage the Tennessee.[13]

Chief Engineer Mortimer Kellogg, Steam Log, USS *Brooklyn*

At 3 o'clock called all hands and prepared to get underway. Fires banked, distilling water for ship's use. At 5 o'clock spread fires, fill oil cups, moved engines. At 5:12 a.m. placed all engineer's department at quarters. Hove up anchor and started ahead slow, with the U.S. gunboat Octorara lashed to out port side. At 5:40 beat to quarters for general action. The Brooklyn was heading up the channel, followed by the rest of the fleet. Moved the engine first slow, stopped, and back quite frequently in accordance with bell signals from the deck. From 7:15 to 7:30 close under and abreast the water batteries of Fort Morgan and receiving rapid and sharp firing from the batteries of the fort and from the rebel ram Tennessee came to anchor in Mobile Bay at 8:05 a.m.[14]

6

Commander Profiles

Engineer and inventor John Ericsson was born in 1808 in the Swedish province of Langbanshyttan, Vermland, and joined the Swedish army at the age of seventeen. He worked on topographical surveying for the army. He moved to London in 1826 and had many engineering projects, including all types of steam-powered engines and locomotives, and he developed improved propeller designs. Perhaps Ericsson's boldest invention was the screw propeller (U.S. patent no. 588), which is still the main form of marine propulsion.

His next move was to New York City in 1839, "where he and Captain Robert Stockton designed the U.S. Navy's first screw-powered warship." Ericsson became a U.S. citizen on October 28, 1848. With the outbreak of the American Civil War, President Abraham Lincoln signed Bill No. 36 into law, establishing the Ironclad Board, authorizing $1.5 million for the construction of ironclad warships. "He [Ericsson] designed and built the *Monitor* for the Union Navy in one hundred working days, however the *Monitor* was not the first ironclad warship; the French and English had launched armor plated warships prior to the construction of the *Monitor*. Ericsson's contract stipulated that if his design failed, he would have to return his payment for the ship to the U.S. government. The Confederate navy, as small as it was, put ironclads into service long before the Yankees got around to it."[1]

Of the sixty monitors built, thirty-seven were commissioned, including the *Tecumseh*. The *Passaic* and *Canonicus* monitors were larger and had

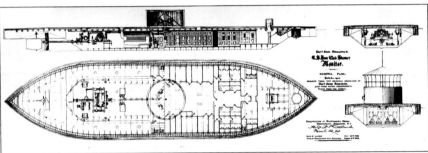

Top, left: Swedish engineer and inventor John Ericsson (July 31, 1803–March 8, 1889) was invaluable as a shipbuilder and inventor. Born in 1808 in Langbanshyttan, Vermland, he had many engineering projects. *U.S. Naval Historical Center NH 305.*

Top, right: Secretary of the Navy Gideon Welles (July 1, 1802–February 11, 1878). He was actively involved with overseeing the growth of the Union navy from 42 ships in 1861 to 675 at the end of the war, resulting in the largest navy in the world. *Library of Congress.*

Bottom: Ericsson's monitor. *U.S. Navy Art Collection: NH 50954.*

many improvements over the original USS *Monitor* of Hampton Roads fame. Commodore Joseph Smith of the Ironclad Board suggested the new monitors have thicker hull plating, better steering, larger guns and improved pilothouse design, to name a few features. Ericsson went to work, and the new Passaic class was larger—two hundred feet by forty-five feet—and the hull had a shiplike design with a rounder hull. But the biggest improvement was that the pilothouse was enlarged to six feet in diameter and mounted on top of the turret.[2] Ericsson did not approve of double-turreted ironclads, because they limited the turning radius of the guns.

In September 1862, Ericsson was called upon to consider the problem of removing Confederate obstructions, including torpedoes, that had been placed in the rivers to prevent Union warships from running past Fort McAllister and Charleston Harbor. Ericsson proposed using a raft pushed by a monitor carrying an explosive charge on its bow to blow up these obstructions. Assistant Secretary of the Navy Gustavus Fox ordered four rafts and thirty charges to be built under the supervision of U.S. Navy chief engineer Alban C. Stimers.

After the war, Ericsson built monitor-type vessels for other countries, including gunboats for Spain. He also built a "torpedo boat" in 1878 that could outrun ironclads and could partly submerge to fire a torpedo projectile underwater. The *Destroyer*, however, never gained the interest of the U.S. Navy. Ericsson died in New York City on March 8, 1889.

GIDEON WELLES

Gideon Welles served as United States Secretary of the Navy from 1861 to 1869. Although opposed to blockading Southern ports, "Father Neptune," as Lincoln nicknamed him, carried out his duties as his position required. In 1861, Welles found the Naval Department "in disarray with Southern officers resigning en masse."[3] His first major action, under President Lincoln's instructions, was to order the USS *Powhatan*, the navy's most powerful warship, to relieve Fort Sumter. However, Secretary of State William Henry Seward ordered the *Powhatan* to Fort Pickins at Pensacola, Florida. "Several weeks later, when Steward argued for a blockade of Southern ports, Welles argued vociferously against the action....Welles was overruled by Lincoln. Despite his misgivings, Welles' efforts to rebuild the Navy and implement the blockade proved extraordinarily effective."[4]

Beginning the war with 42 ships in 1861, the Union navy eventually grew to 675, the largest navy in the world. "Despite his success, Welles was never at ease in the Cabinet. After Lincoln's assassination, he was retained by President Andrew Johnson as Secretary of the Navy and in 1866 Welles and Seward, were instrumental in launching the National Union Party as a third party."[5]

"The much-heralded duel between the *Monitor* and the *Merrimack* [CSS *Virginia*] had produced a veritable monitor craze throughout the North."[6]

Admiral David Glasgow Farragut

At the age of seven, when his mother died, James Glasgow Farragut was sent to live with David Porter to learn the ways of the sea and was adopted by the Porter family. Out of respect to Porter, Farragut changed his first name from James to David.

"In April, 1862 while commander of the West Gulf Blockading Squadron, Flag Officer Farragut took the city and port of New Orleans."[7]

He was awarded the rank of rear admiral, the first in the Union navy. Two months later, he was unsuccessful in taking Vicksburg and was forced to withdraw. In 1863, Farragut was also unsuccessful at Port Hudson. General Nathaniel Banks had planned the attack to begin on the morning of March 15, 1863, but Farragut began on the evening on the fourteenth. The fleet was forced to retreat with many casualties.

Farragut finally redeemed himself on August 5, 1864, by leading his van of ships into Mobile Bay. Admiral Farragut was a very different person from the man of determined nature at the war's beginning. He was promoted to the rank of vice admiral and offered command of the North Atlantic Fleet but declined due to "mental strain and fatigue."

Confederate sergeant Robert B. Tarpley wrote in his diary about Farragut: "Six months constantly watching day and night for an enemy; to know him to be brave, as skillful and determined as myself, who [had] pledged to his government and the South to drive me away and raise the blockade."[8]

U.S. Flagship Hartford
Mobile Bay, September 5, 1864

As my work appears to be at an end for the time I shall ask a respite from duty, as I have not felt well lately. I never was in favor of taking Mobile, except for the moral effect, as I believe it would be used by our own people to flood rebeldom with all their supplies. I am confining them pretty strictly to the limits of their city, so far as the bay is concerned.

Wishing you every success, I remain, very respectfully, your obedient servant,[9]

D.G. Farragut,
Rear Admiral

Rear Admiral David Glasgow Farragut (July 5, 1801–August 14, 1870), commander of the Union fleet and commander of the fleet at the Battle of Mobile Bay, August 5, 1864. *National Archives (NAID 529975).*

CONFIDENTIAL.] HDQRS. Mil. Div. of West Mississippi
New Orleans, La., September 15, 1864
Rear Admiral D.G. Farragut,
Comdg. West Gulf Blocking Squadron, Mobile Bay, Ala.

ADMIRAL: …I propose to send a force back to Mobile Bay for the purpose of operating up the Alabama River, directing the first operations against the works on Spanish and Tensas Rivers, with the expectation of getting control of these rivers and affecting a lodgment on the Alabama at or near Fort Stoddard. This I think will force the rebels to abandon Mobile…[10]

Admiral Farragut appears to have had a deep-rooted and ineradicable dislike, and even contempt, for ironclads, and his feelings in regard to them are often expressed in language that is both vigorous and comical. Writing from Pensacola on August 21, 1862, he said: 'We have no dread of rams or he-goats and if our editors had less, the country would be better off. Now they scare everybody to death. The ironclads are cowardly things, and I don't want them to succeed in the world."[11]

COMMANDER TUNIS AUGUSTUS MACDONOUGH CRAVEN

Tunis Craven graduated from the Partridge School, entered the navy as a midshipman in 1826 and was promoted to lieutenant in the war with Mexico. In 1859, he was appointed captain of the steamer *Mohawk* off the coast of Florida.

Promoted to commander in 1861, he took command of the USS *Tecumseh* and joined Farragut in Mobile Bay to lead the column of warships past Fort Morgan. He fired the first shot to open the operations to close the port of Mobile and capture the forts. When *Tecumseh* hit the torpedo, Craven and his pilot were scrambling to exit the turret through the narrow hatch. They met there at the bottom of the ladder at the same time. Craven stepped aside and said to the pilot, "You first, sir." The monitor began to roll and take on water fast; Craven went down with the ship along with ninety-three others.

Earlier, Craven had made several recommendations concerning *Tecumseh*. He suggested that all battle hatches have hinges and that the two gun ports have a four-and-three-fourths-inch gap between the muzzle and the port sill. He also recommended that the gun ports be the same size. In addition, the anchor windlass was slow and cumbersome and took two

Left: Tunis Augustus Macdonough Craven (January 11, 1813–August 5, 1864), commander, USS *Tecumseh*. *Astle-Alpaugh Family Foundation.*

Right: Commander Percival Drayton (August 25, 1812–August 4, 1865), U.S. Navy, USS *Hartford*. Letters From Captain Percival Drayton, 1851–1865.

hours to heave forty-five fathoms of chain. Craven believed it should take no more than forty-five minutes.

COMMANDER PERCIVAL DRAYTON, U.S. NAVY

Commander Drayton was born in Charleston, South Carolina, and initially served on the frigate USS *Hudson* in the South Atlantic. His older brother, Thomas, was a graduate of West Point, but he resigned his commission and became a general in the Confederate army.

As a career United States Navy officer, Drayton served as Farragut's fleet captain during the war and was given command of the ironclad USS *Passaic*. Working with engineer John Ericsson, he assisted in overseeing the outfitting and design of the vessel in September 1862. In December 1863, Drayton began a year as fleet captain to the West Gulf Blockading Squadron and commander of Farragut's flagship, USS *Hartford*.

In April 1865, Drayton was appointed chief of the Bureau of Navigation. He died on August 4, 1865, in Washington, D.C.

Admiral Franklin Buchanan

Having served in the United States Navy for forty-five years, Buchanan had extensive and worldwide sea duty. He commanded the *Vincennes* and *Germantown* during the 1840s and the frigate *Susquehanna* from 1852 to 1854. He served as the first Superintendent of the United States Naval Academy. From 1859 until 1861, he was commandant of the Washington Navy Yard. On April 22, 1861, Buchanan resigned his captain's commission and joined the Confederate navy on February 24, 1862.[12]

Stephen Mallory appointed Buchanan as flag officer of the James River Squadron, and he was selected to command the new ironclad CSS *Virginia* as his flagship. While engaging the USS *Congress*, Buchanan was wounded by a Minié ball in the thigh that kept him from commanding the *Virginia* against the USS *Monitor*. In August 1862, he was promoted to the only full admiral in the Confederate navy.

"Buchanan was sent to command the Confederate naval forces stationed in Mobile Bay and he oversaw the construction of his new ironclad, CSS *Tennessee* as its keel was laid in October 1862. When Farragut's vanguard overtook Fort Morgan and entered the upper bay, on August 5, and engaged the *Tennessee*, Buchanan was severely wounded and taken prisoner. He was finally exchanged in February 1865."[13] After the war, he lived in Mobile until 1870, when he took up final residence in Maryland.

Major General Dabney Herndon Maury

"Dabney Maury born in Fredericksburg, Virginia, the son of Naval Lieutenant John Minor Maury who died of yellow fever in the West Indies when Dabney was only two, and was brought up by his uncle Matthew Fontaine Maury known as the 'Father of Modern Oceanography and Meteorology.'"[14]

Maury was an officer in the United States Army, instructor at West Point, author of military training books and a major general in the Confederate States Army during the Civil War.[15] Maury served as a lieutenant in the United States Army from 1846 until he resigned his commission in 1861 to become a colonel in the Confederate army. Maury served as adjutant general and served under General Earl Van Dorn as his chief of staff. "In 1868 he organized the Southern Historical Society in Richmond, Virginia where he spent 20 years working for the Society that produced

Left: Admiral Franklin Buchanan (September 13, 1800–May 11, 1874), Confederate navy, commander of CSS *Tennessee*. Buchanan, *Confederate Admiral: The Life and Wars of Franklin Buchanan*.

Right: Confederate major general Dabney Herndon Maury (May 21, 1822–January 11, 1900). *Recollections of a Virginian in the Mexican, Indian and Civil Wars*.

52 volumes of Southern history and genealogy. With the conclusion of the Civil War, Maury came home to Virginia and established an academy in Fredericksburg to teach classical literature and mathematics."[16]

STEPHEN RUSSELL MALLORY

"Mallory was a Democrat in the United States Senate from Florida from 1850 until the secession of his home state and the outbreak of the Civil War."[17] As chairman of the Committee on Naval Affairs, Mallory considered it was time to update the U.S. Navy into a formable force, as had Britain and France. Mallory left the Union when he was named secretary of the Confederate navy by President Jefferson Davis.

"Because of indifference to naval matters by most others in the Confederacy, Mallory was able to shape the Confederate Navy according to the principles he had learned while serving in the US Senate. Some of his ideas, such as the incorporation of armor into warship construction, were quite successful and became standard in navies around the world."[18]

However, the navy was often handicapped by administrative incompetence in the Navy Department.

In a statement made by Mallory, he was very forthright in his opinion of ironclads over wooden ships:

> *I regard possession of iron-armored ship as a matter of the first necessity. Such a vessel at this time could traverse the entire coast of the United States, prevent all blockades, and encounter with a fair prospect of success, their entire navy. If, to cope with them upon the sea, we follow their example, and build wooden ships, we shall have to construct several at one time, for one or two ships would fall an easy prey to their comparatively numerous steam frigates. But inequality of numbers may be compensated by invulnerability, and thus not only does economy, but naval success dictate the wisdom and expediency of fighting with iron against wood without regard first cost.*

After the war, the Confederate government fled from Richmond. Mallory was investigated, but the committee found no evidence of his wrongdoing, although several members of his cabinet were charged with treason and sent to prison.

7

NEWSPAPER PRESS REPORTS

OPERATION TECUMSEH

Smithsonian Team Seeks Famed Civil War Vessel
Bay Searched for Trace of Union Ship Tecumseh
Ed Lee, Mobile Press, _Thursday, January 12, 1967:_
The first shot has been fired in the second Battle of Mobile Bay. A team is searching the bottom off Fort Morgan today, attempting to locate the wreckage of the Tecumseh which was sunk during the Civil War Battle of Mobile Bay on August 5, 1864. Colonel Robert M. Calland (U.S. Marine Corps (retired)) staff member of the Armed Forces Museum proposed branch of the Smithsonian Institute from Washington, D.C., is in charge of the search.[1]

Secret of Tecumseh Revealed
Bill Sellers, Mobile Press, _Saturday Morning, February 18, 1967:_
The searchers and would-be salvagers were bewildered by the fact that no clear sign could be found of the 225 foot warship which had unique superstructure and should have been only a dozen or so feet beneath the water's surface. The mystery was solved with week....The secret was the fact that the ship had rolled over while sinking and came to rest with the keel up and the superstructure going into the mud, silt and sand.[2]

Ed Lee, Mobile Press Register, *Sunday, February 19, 1967:*
Friday's official announcement of the discovery of the Civil War Tecumseh in lower Mobile Bay was good news along the waterfront. Speculation now is what may still be aboard the Union ironclad sent to the bottom 103 years ago.[3]

There were two theories concerning the "tower thing." One held that it was a lost World War II German submarine that was rumored to have been sunk in the bay. Another theory held that the remains were of H.L. Hunley's experimental submarine (*Pioneer II*). Of course, neither was correct.

Court Cases Over Ownership and Salvage Rights
Smithsonian Seeking to Salvage Tecumseh
Mobile Press, *Friday Morning, March 10, 1967:*
The Army Corps of Engineers in Mobile has received an application from the Smithsonian Institution to raise the Union ironclad Tecumseh from its century old resting place in lower Mobile Bay, the Mobile District office said Thursday. Protest against the dredging and salvage work must be filed in the district office by March 18....The U.S. Navy proposes to raise the Civil War vessel and place it in a museum in Washington. A man in Mobile, J.O. Wintzell, Jr. filed suit in Circuit Court at Mobile asking that the Smithsonian be barred from raising and taking possession of the ironclad. No hearing date has been set. Wintzell claims he discovered Tecumseh's location and registered it with the State of Alabama in February 1965. He contends the state gave him salvage rights.[4]

Tecumseh Suit Hearing Date Expected Today
Mobile Press, *Friday Evening, March 10, 1967:*
Attorney M.A. Marsal said he hopes to have a hearing date set on a suit filed in Circuit Court to prevent the Smithsonian Institute from raising the Civil War ironclad Tecumseh from Mobile Bay. The lawyer, who represents J.O. Wintzell Jr. said he expects to have a court order to forbid the ship's salvage before March 18, the deadline for protest.[5]

War for Tecumseh Opens
Harry McDonnell, Mobile Press Register, *March 16, 1967:*
The State of Alabama, through the Conservation Department, opened fire today on the Smithsonian Institution's plan to raise the ironclad monitor

Tecumseh…and take it to Washington. Claude D. Kelley, director of the State Department of Conservation, today filed a formal protest with the U.S. Corps of Engineers to the Smithsonian's plan to remove the historic vessel to the Armed Forces Museum. Kelley cited a legislative act of 1958: "The State of Alabama reserves to itself the exclusive right of and privilege of exploring, excavating or surveying through its authorized officers, agents or employees all aboriginal mounds and other antiquities."[6]

Jaycees Get the Nod
Mobile Press, *March, 1967:*
Mobile businessman, J.O. Wintzell…today said he is turning his claim of salvage rights to the Civil War Union ironclad over to the Mobile Junior Chamber of Commerce. Fred Killion, Jaycee president, said the group plans to work to obtain title to the historic vessel and place it on public display in the Mobile area "for the benefit of this area."

Meanwhile at Montgomery, State Representative Robert Edington said today the State of Alabama stands a better than fair chance of winning a fight to keep Tecumseh in the Mobile area.[7]

Case of Ironclad Tecumseh Transferred to U.S. Court
Ed Lee, Mobile Press, *Saturday Morning, March 25, 1967:*
U.S. District Attorney, Vernol Jansen Jr. filed the motion of removal in Federal Court Friday afternoon asking for the action since agencies and employees of the government are involved. The suit also involved the U.S. Navy and the Army [Corps of Engineers]. *A motion to remove a case to federal court on such grounds is automatic.*[8]

Ship Salvage in News Now; Bulletin Gives Few Points
Ed Lee, Mobile Press Register, *Sunday, March 26, 1967:*
This article is very complex in its attempt to explain all the ramifications of the many maritime laws in existence in 1967. It discusses the U.S. Coast Guard's Law Bulletin No. 314 of April 1962. Under this law, "to salvage a sunken ship, the salvor does not become the owner of the rescued property, but he does automatically receive a salvage lien on that property, such a lien gives the salvor the right to hold the property but the owner could regain his property either by agreeing to a satisfactory reward or in lieu of that, by posting a security bond either a surety bond, cash or other collateral."[9]

This is just one example of the many complications concerning rights, title and interest in salvage of shipwrecks within the boundaries of the United States.

Can't Move Tecumseh
Press Capital Bureau *(Montgomery, AL), March 27, 1967:*
Several important decisions concerning claims were reported today attempting to resolve some of the claims to Tecumseh. Claude Kelly, State Conservation Director, turned down J.O. Wintzell's request for a permit to remove Tecumseh from Mobile Bay. Kelly also stated; "his department, for the time being will issue no permits for salvage activity on the Union warship."[10]

In another action sponsored by State Representative Robert Edington, would create a committee to seek a compromise solution to the salvage controversy. "The resolution was approved by the House and sent to the Senate more than a week ago."[11]

Fight Rages on Ironclad
Mobile Press, *Tuesday, March 28, 1967:*
U.S. Attorney Vernol R. Jansen, Jr., today filed a motion to dismiss suit transferred last week from Mobile Circuit Court to federal court to prevent federal agencies from salvaging the Tecumseh.

Representatives of the Smithsonian Institution have announced to raise and preserve the Civil War ironclad warship....[12]

Cairo Saga Might Be Text for Decision on Tecumseh
Ed Lee, Mobile Press Register, *Sunday, April 2, 1967:*
Ideas are mixed on who should be granted rights, but all agree that the job of raising the old historic Union warship should not be undertaken until sufficient funds are available to do the job right. Let's not find ourselves in the same shape as Mississippi with the Cairo. That is, have a vessel raised, and three years later still not know where the money will come from to complete the job of providing the ship as a tourist attraction. We might add that it took four tries to raise the Cairo. The first three ended in failure and there's no record of what they cost.[13]

Won't Give Up the Ship
Mobile Press, *Thursday, May 18, 1967:*
U.S. District Judge Daniel H. Thomas dismissed J.O. Wintzell's suit. If an amended complaint is not filed by the date set by the court (May 31),

no similar suit may be filed later, the court order said. The Smithsonian, who obtained title to the Tecumseh from the U.S. Navy, proposes to raise the ironclad and place it on display in a Washington museum. However, U.S. Attorney Vernol R. Jansen Jr. contended the ship was the property of the federal government and further argued that a branch of the federal government, the Smithsonian could not be sued to keep it from taking possession.[14]

SUMMARY

With all lawsuits and ownership resolved, "Operation *Tecumseh*" could begin as planned. In June 1964, Jack A. Friend presented his report, "Preliminary Considerations: The Salvage, Preservation and Display of the U.S.S. Tecumseh" to the legislative committee on the *Tecumseh*. In his twenty-five page report, precise measures were addressed and the concept for Bicentennial Park, the Smithsonian's National Armed Forces Historical Museum Park, the new home of *Tecumseh*.[15]

Dr. John Nicholas Brown
Chairman, National Armed Forces Museum Advisory Board
50 South Main Street
Providence, Rhode Island

Dear John,
I am pleased to advise you that the Board of Regents of the Smithsonian Institution considered the suggested change in the name National Armed Forces Historical Park. A vote by mail ballot resulted in the approval of the following motion:
    VOTED that the Board of Regents approves the change in name of the National Armed Forces Historical Museum Park to "Bicentennial Park."

With all good wishes,
Sincerely yours,
S. Dillon
Secretary
3-23-70

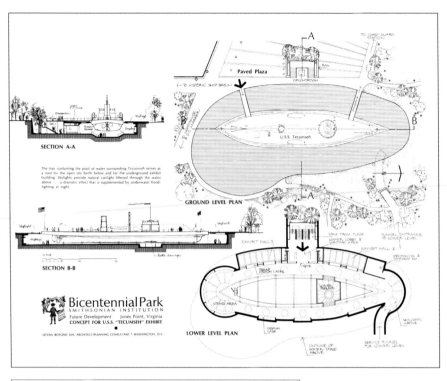

IN REPLY REFER TO
SAMOP-S   8 March 1967

TO WHOM IT MAY CONCERN:

This District has received application for a permit to dredge and conduct salvage work in a navigable waterway as follows:

Applicant: Smithsonian Institution
                  Washington, D. C. 20560

Waterway: Mobile Bay

Work: Raise the USS TECUMSEH from Mobile Bay position Latitude 30°13'36", Longitude 88°1'45". The salvage work will include dredging approximately 22,650 cu. yds. of material from the bottom at this location and/depositing it in deep open water.

Any protests or objections against this work must be received at the office of the District Engineer, Room 13, Building 2, 2301 Airport Boulevard, Mobile, Alabama, not later than 18 March 1967; otherwise, it will be considered that there is no objection.

For accuracy and completeness of the record, all data in support of or in opposition to the proposed work should be submitted in writing setting forth sufficient detail to furnish a clear understanding of the reasons for support or opposition. While a Department of the Army permit merely expresses assent so far as the public rights of navigation are concerned, information from interested persons on aspects of the proposed work other than navigation will be accepted and made a part of the record on the application. In cases of conflicting property rights, the Corps of Engineers cannot undertake to settle rival claims.

JOSEPH D. BENNETT
LTC, Corps of Engineers
Deputy District Engineer

Above: Proposed display of *Tecumseh* for the National Armed Forces Museum Park, Washington, D.C. *Smithsonian Institution.*

Left: Concept for Bicentennial Park exhibit of *Tecumseh. Istvan Botond, AIA Architect Planning Consultant, Washington, D.C.*

Opposite, top: Smithsonian Institution Press Release #1. *Smithsonian Institution.*

Opposite, bottom: Smithsonian Institution Press Release #2. *Smithsonian Institution, Colonel John H. Magruder III, U.S. Marine Corps.*

SMITHSONIAN ⬤ INSTITUTION

NEWS SERVICE: 381-5143

PRESS RELEASE

For Release: April 19, 1965

SMITHSONIAN STUDY TAPS FORT WASHINGTON
FOR NATIONAL ARMED FORCES MUSEUM SITE

WASHINGTON, D.C.--Secretary S. Dillon Ripley today issued a Smithsonian Institution study recommending the establishment of a National Armed Forces Museum situated on a 340-acre tract bordering the Potomac River at Fort Washington, Md., 25 minutes from the center of the Nation's Capital.

The detailed study, undertaken by the National Armed Forces Museum Advisory Board, emphasized that the proposed museum, as conceived by Congress, represents:

"a dramatically new approach to the documentation of history. In concept the museum would seek to inspire the public with a meaningful sense of the accomplishments of the Nation's Armed Forces, their contributions to national development, and the role played by our people in providing the sinews of defense for maintaining a free, peaceful, and independent society and culture in the United States of America."

Graphically described would be not only the Armed Forces achievements in war but also their extensive peacetime contributions in fields such as science, nuclear energy, terrestrial and space exploration, electronics, engineering, aeronautics, and medicine. Dramatic displays would afford interpretation of significant current problems affecting national security.

The new museum would entail a park complex embracing reconstructions of fortifications, earthworks, trenches, and other military and naval facilities characteristic of memorable periods in our Nation's history; a ship basin in which to preserve and exhibit significant specimens of naval vessels; and outdoor displays of large military objects unsuited to indoor exhibit.

A large parade ground would accommodate parades, tattoos, military re-enactments, and similar spectacles. A central exhibit building, specially designed to house large pieces of military equipment, would include a study center for scholarly research into the meaning of war and its effect on civilization.

Bands, high-school cadets, and ROTC units would be encouraged to use the parade ground for drill competitions. Reconstructions of military encampments would provide opportunities for Boy Scouts to experience a weekend or more of camp routine, while Sea Scouts could be treated to a taste of shipboard life by dockside cruises aboard one of the naval vessels.

The very nature of the museum, the Advisory Board observed, would tend to attract visitors for a full day's excursion. Exhibits would be merged with the natural setting of the park, with full provision being made for picnic and recreation areas and adequate parking and restaurant facilities. Automobile and bus traffic would be controlled so as to prevent its intrusion on the park, with a trackless train shuttling visitors from a reception center to the exhibit and recreational areas.

Selection of Fort Washington, up the Potomac some three miles from Mount Vernon, was based on several factors: it offers sufficient acreage to permit construction of buildings and outdoor displays; room for large numbers of visitors; accessibility to existing highways and close proximity to the District of Columbia; diversity of natural terrain; and water frontage offering convenient access to deep draft vessels.

The Advisory Board also noted that Fort Washington already possesses many facilities that could be readily incorporated in the National Armed Forces Museum plan at considerable budgetary saving. These include existing examples of fortifications spanning nearly 125 years of the Nation's history, as well as a ready-made network of roads and park facilities.

"Finally," the study noted, "since Fort Washington is owned by the Federal Government (National Park Service), its selection would eliminate the need of acquiring additional land in an area of steadily mounting property values."

Other sites investigated by the Board but turned down include the Naval Air Station-Bolling Field-Anacostia area and the Naval Weapons Plant, all in the District of Columbia; the Fort Foote-Smoot Bay area, Maryland; and Hallowing Point and Jones Point, both in Virginia.

Members of the National Armed Forces Museum Advisory Board include John Nicholas Brown, Chairman; Chief Justice Earl Warren; David L. Kreeger; Henry B. Washburn, jr.; William H. Perkins, Jr.; James S. Cassell, Jr.; Secretary of the Army, Stephen Ailes; Secretary of the Navy, Paul H. Nitze; and Secretary of the Air Force, Eugene M. Zuckert. Secretary of Defense, Robert S. McNamara, and S. Dillon Ripley, Secretary of the Smithsonian, serve as ex-officio members.

The detailed study was coordinated under the direction of Col. John H. Magruder, III, of the U.S. Marine Corps.

8

1967 SMITHSONIAN INSTITUTION SURVEY
AND DIVE NOTES

W hile serving as president, Dwight D. Eisenhower became convinced that the establishment of a National Armed Forces Museum could make a substantial contribution to our citizens' understanding of American life. He appointed Chief Justice Earl Warren as chairman of a committee to formulate plans to create the museum under the auspices of the Smithsonian Institution. In 1969, the plan to establish the park was recommended to Congress and became Public Law 87-186 on August 30, 1961.

> *In the summer of 1965, the National Armed Forces Museum Advisory Board (NAFMAB) realized there was an interest in recovering Tecumseh by private individuals. Realizing the potential of the ironclad for display at the National Armed Forces Museum Park, the Smithsonian initiated a feasibility study for its recovery. As an initial step, title to the vessel was transferred from the General Services Administration to the Smithsonian Institution on June 3, 1966.*[1]

As a monument to our naval heritage, *Tecumseh* would have opened new avenues to learn about the technology and innovations that revolutionized ship construction and naval warfare in the nineteenth century. This project would also give an opportunity to study the long-term effects of being submerged in salt water for one hundred years as well as restoration and preservation techniques.

In 1969, project historian James J. Stokesberry produced a twenty-four-page report, "USS Tecumseh: Capsule of History," outlining future operations of the project. Tecumseh's salvage was to be accomplished in four phases:

PHASE I. De-silting and cleaning out of the hull (including the removal of all artifacts and heavy equipment such as coal, ordnance and miscellaneous stores) and the recovery and interment of human remains.

PHASE II. The raising and righting of the hull and its delivery to a temporary berth in the Mobile area.

PHASE III. The cleaning, preservation and restoration of the hull and its components.

PHASE IV. Movement of the vessel to the Potomac River for permanent display in the National Armed Forces Historical Museum Park.[2]

Jim Smith, in a report to the commission, wrote, "From a technical point of view Tecumseh offers rare opportunities for expanding our knowledge of ship salvage, the effects of salt water on numerous materials after prolonged submersion, underwater archaeology and restoration and preservation techniques."[3]

"In early January 1967, after securing title to *Tecumseh*, from the United States Government, a team of Smithsonian and Navy salvage personnel

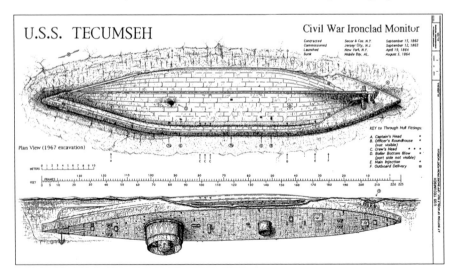

USS *Tecumseh* Reference Chart. *Frame 93 91 89. Martin D. Peoples, 15 July 1995, Historic American Engineering Record AL-124.*

Aerial view of *Tecumseh* site during Smithsonian Project. *Smithsonian Institution SIA 2020-002839.tif.*

made an initial attempt to locate *Tecumseh* by dragging a cable behind two boats in an area in which the monitor was known to have sunk."[4]

Unfortunately, it was assumed the monitor was upright, and the cable was planned to snag the turret. Unable to locate the site by this method, it called into question whether the official records were correct. On February 1, 1967, a new search was made by the Western Instrument Corporation using modern electronic equipment designed to detect underwater metal objects. Finally, a navy diver was lowered to the bottom after a large metal mass was detected in the primary search area. It was then they realized that the monitor was upside down and completely covered with sand and mud.

Members of the original Smithsonian Tecumseh Project team, including project manager Colonel Robert M. Calland (USMC, Ret.), project historian James Stokesberry, navy supervisor of salvage Willard F. Searle Jr. (USN, Ret.), diver Earl Lawrence and Smithsonian museum specialist Jim Hutchins, provided firsthand accounts of the work at the site and were able to fill in many of the puzzling gaps in the historical record.

"External examination of the hull and an analysis of specimens of iron plating and frame sections removed by divers have shown that the hull is in amazingly good condition. *Tecumseh* appears to have been covered almost from the moment she reached the bottom, preserved from encroachment by sea and man."[5]

This report, providing a detailed technical description of the monitor USS
Tecumseh, *is designed to serve three purposes:*
1) To enable positive identification of the wreck.
2) To assist in evaluating the present strength and condition of the hull and
   to guide divers and other technicians during salvage operations.
3) To assist in restoring the vessel as much as possible to her original battle-
   ready condition on that fateful day; August 5, 1864.[6]

The first two purposes were completed, but not the third.

NOTE: The following are excerpts from the ninety-nine pages of the dive log
covering the two weeks of exploration, July 7–July 23, 1967. Some entries
have been edited for a clearer understanding.

Day One: Friday, July 7, 1967 (CALLAND)

Operation Tecumseh got underway when Colonel Robert M. Calland
(U.S. Marine Corps, retired), staff member of the Armed Forces
Museum proposed branch of the Smithsonian Institution in Washington,
D.C. and dive master Earl Lawrence assembled the dive team on the site
of Tecumseh. The investigation and survey was planned to take in three
stages: identification, evaluation and restoration. The 99 page dive log
book is full of measurements and details of the torpedo damage that took
her down. A hull model was used to locate and mark important features to
be investigated during the operations. A scale was made of the model with
225 feet of length on one side and a "frame" scale of 140.15 on the
other for reference. The estimated exposed area, the area initially exposed,
has been marked on the hull model dated 7 July 1967 and buoy #1 also
located on the model. These marks are in green grease pencil.
    The dive team consisted of Buster Miller's crew including S.I. Miller,
J. Ray Miller, J.F. Miller, and George Hall. A voice communications
system was used with divers having direct contact with topside at all
times and the communications were recorded in the dive log. During the
fourteen day explorations the average bottom time was twelve hours per
day which produced over 160 dive hours. A real calm day with a little
bit of visibility. The first buoy has been marked and our next plan is to
mark both ends of the ship so we can get the proper lay of the whole thing.

Left: A suited-up diver on deck preparing to dive. *Smithsonian Institution SIA 2020-00841.tif.*

Right: Diver returning from dive. *Smithsonian Institution SIA 2020-002842.tif.*

Earl Lawrence is acting as salvage master on this operation. S.L. Miller has assembled a diving barge completely fitted with air lift, top side air, welding equipment, cutting torches and all the equipment that is anticipated we will need in this uncovering and hull inspection.

The tide is going out at excessive rates. It is impractical to try to continue any cleaning operations or further marking.[7]

Day Two: Saturday, July 8 (CALLAND/WARD/LAWRENCE)

The air lift was sent down to attempt to clean out mud and silt from inside the hole discovered the previous day to determine the contents of this compartment and to determine the dimensions so as to further locate the hole relative to the frame number on the model. Fred Ward, National Geographic photographer, was picked up at the airport on Dauphin Island and taken by boat to the site to take still photographs of the underwater operations while Englund Flying Service made 10 aerial passes over the barge photographing the site.

A lot of silt in the water and the tide ran out the entire day yesterday, some times running up to 3 knots making diving difficult and visibility extremely poor.

There is a small hole by the—on the top of the hull. Divers report on site visibility is 18 inches and for the past hour been investigating the metal around this hole area. I took a four pound hammer and chopped the scale over the outer side of the hole which was approximately ½ inch thick then reached on the inside of the hole and beat off the scale on the underneath side and cleaned an area probably 12 inches long by 6 inches wide. Metal seemed to be real solid under the scale.

Located turret with an 11 foot piece of ¾ inch pipe—probed 20 times—turret is in place.[8]

————

Day Three: Sunday, July 9 (CALLAND/B. MILLER)

All crew members on board. Jack Elliott from the Smithsonian is due to arrive today from Washington, D.C. for the specific purpose of monitoring the dredging discharge when we start the large dredge probably on Tuesday.

The weather today is ideal temperature is 70 degrees, wind is off shore and the water surface is mirror-like.

Miller was down with water-jet hoses washing in the vicinity of the turret to the air lift for removal.

We have now a little more geography on the ship itself. We know now that we determined this morning that the hole, which is our reference point for all washing, was somewhere between frame 86 and 88. Further washing around the ship uncovered the mooring of a recess just inside the armor belt approximately one foot from the gunnels, eight inches in diameter recessed about five inches. This corresponds with the mooring devices shown on the general plan of a Tippecanoe class of monitors. Several items of interest: she is in mud, not sand or silt, actually black mud. At the elevation of the deck line, I found grass and small limbs and other debris indicating that at one time she was at the bottom of the adjacent area.

I also found attached to the deck some oyster shells which indicate that at one time this has been sunk and the water level, the mud line was such that you had water there and the oysters were able to attach themselves and grow. Because of the nature of the material that I find as I wash it away, I am of the opinion that all the materials are moving now are materials since this vessel went down.[9]

[Off Monday, July 10]

———

Day Four: Tuesday, July 11 (MILLER/LAWRENCE/ELLIOTT)

Jack Elliott on board joining the crew to over-see area of discharge of spoil from dredge in case we run into any loose artifacts or other materials we want to salvage. Just been advised the dredge would be delayed one day in arriving from New Orleans because of local problems beyond their control.

We have completed the planned preliminary diving operations to prepare for the arrival of the dredge. When the dredge gets here and sets up and starts pumping, our first plan is to work on the inboard side and clear away primarily large masses of material so we can expose the bottom of the ship to get a chance to work the whole area foot by foot to determine the condition and start our plan of where we will take samples.

Taking samples; the laboratory will receive one foot squares to be examined by cutting the metal into two inch strips which they will bend, pull and subject to numerous stresses in their analysis of strength. Taking a sample from the skin can be immediately and easily patched. These samples will be taken from places that will not mar the general appearance of the ship or they stand historically as sampled areas. It is quite possible that these, being temporary patches that a later date if desirable that repair could be glossed over and made more invisible or less visible.

Mr. E.P. Gavin and Mr. Todd Witt from Ramset Division of Olin are here for consultation and possible assistance in tapping the hull for air samples. An assistant engineer, Mr. J.W. Rawson is also on board seeking information concerning arrival of the dredge Janhki from New Orleans.

Anchors have been repositioned and the barge located to accommodate the dredge which is expected later this afternoon. At 2:40 p.m. the dredge arrived and is positioned 1000 yards to the west of us. At 9:30 p.m. dredge is in position.[10]

———

Day Five: Wednesday, July 12 (B. Miller/G. Hall/ Butler)

The weather today: we have some low hanging clouds south and east of us and a southeasterly breeze at about 12 to 15 knots, temperature about 70.

There are much the same clouds as yesterday morning but we missed any rain. There is a slight two or three foot chop on the water.

The dredge *Janhki* from New Orleans positioning a barge for loading debris. *SIA 2020-002840.tif.*

The dredge started pumping at first light this morning and immediately ran into difficulties with the rubber boot projecting out over the suction end. The rubber just collapsed went right up in the tube in the suction end and prevented any pumping. (A long discussion of the problem and its repairs went on for the next several hours).

We seem to be pulling this black ooze right off the top of the sand at a depth of about 35 feet. Working at the rudder level and stern end of the ship, however; as we move amidships and by the curve of the ship being deeper in the sand, we will probably have to go down and the dredge level will be around 40 feet.

We are going to hold off taking any samples of metal, wood or possible air for another two or three days until we have initial survey and a valuation of the integrity of this hull at which point we will then make out a sample-taking plan as far as the external part of the ship is concerned. We have not yet found an opening that would accommodate entry. That is still to be determined when we do find out the exact condition of this hull.[11]

———

Day Six: Thursday, July 13 (Lawrence/Calland/Miller)

Earl Lawrence is going down to try to get a line and put a buoy on the end of the keel right over the propeller so we can get a good tight buoy at that point.

The engineer hydro crew is on the job today verifying the ladder depth gage on the dredge so that we will know exactly how deep we are working and they also will start some hydrographic survey of the bottom. The long range view with the hydro crew is that when all the dredging is completed and we are ready to clear the area they will duplicate the soundings, location soundings of their original hydrographic chart and we will then know how much has been moved out. Six months from now or a year from now we can repeat those soundings and find out how much has washed back in.

Smithsonian photographer, August Stebura, is doing some "catch as catch can" photography and later a little aerial photography. A temporary squall interrupted our work so we batten down for a while.

Just came up from a dive and was able to follow the hull all the way back to the skeg [a seaward extension of the keel that has a rudder mounted on the center line] *to be used as a reference mark. Most of the keel line is now dredged out. Located oblong hole 40 to 50 feet aft from first reported hole that was eight inches wide to ten or 12 inches long.*

Early afternoon, high winds causing six foot waves. The tugs had to immediately go to the pontoon line, get behind it and reinforce it by pushing it into the south west storm. The afternoon was spent fighting the squall and getting pictures showing what the dredge and barge were trying to do to ride it out.

The engineers have just taken a sounding and have a deck at 27 feet and off the deck 37 feet depth, so we have to move quite a bit of dirt out on the shore-ward side of the wreck.

INTERESTING DISCOVERY:

Miller's description and information about the rudder are significant in the fact it confirms the historical account that Captain Craven ordered the vessel's course changed from one of North East to North West, the position of the vessel in the case that—with the rudder in that position, he had entered into the mine field to the west of the buoy marking end of the line of torpedoes. I would like to comment also that the physical layout in the case that no one could possibly conceive that how close the Tecumseh must have seemed to the fort at that time. This is some what special in that the area to the west is rather vast in comparison.

Weather continues to be a significant problem. Until things settle down we were at a stand still.[12]

Day Seven, Friday, July 14 (CALLAND/MILLER)

The weather is still disagreeable so Calland and Miller are reviewing the accounts, contract performance, savings and additions justifying the original contract has been carried out. Before finishing, we received word that the barge was cut loose and is headed for the rocks. We left here in haste. One of the tugs had gone down and was pulling it back out fortunately was pulling it out in time. The engineers had gone aboard, along with the tug crew and had drug it back to safety. The winds had swung around during the night to the north which was the opposite direction and still a good blow but was throwing a chop in another direction. Our barge was pitching heavily also. During the blow we lost all our markings all our buoys, and the only remaining buoy was the Coast Guard buoy.

We received a report that our support boat, the "Suit-Me," had suffered some damage, extent not known at this time. It had to be lifted out of the water to check the bottom. In the meantime, I put in a request to talk to Captain Charter of the Coast Guard and requested the assistance of a boat until "Suit-Me" could be put back into line. They responded by sending launch to Dauphin Island to pick up the photographer and Stokesberry.

We were able to work the bow of the ship and were pretty well cleaned out there. To reach the bow, we had added extra sections of floating line. We were unable to move back toward the stern with these sections of line in there because of the chop and high water. We were unable to break the line and remove sections. The main thing that kept this line in tact was the fact that we were pumping water through it and it gave it weight and once you quit pumping, the water runs out and it becomes like a cork and bobs around.

The engineer survey crew placed long stakes again marking the outline of the ship due to the fact we lost all our markings during the blow.[13]

Day Eight, Saturday, July 15 (CALLAND/LAWRENCE/J. ELLIOTT/MILLER)

Still a steady wind from the north. The contractor's barges, pipeline, extra pipe and work barge have blown ashore up by the Coast Guard pier. Unable to retrieve them yet. Both tugs are required to hold the dredge in place. We spent the morning straightening the diving barge up but it is still tied up to the marina. The dredge is now operating again but there will be no diving today. The wind finally abated and at 4:00 p.m. Lawrence and Miller were over the ship and reported that the hull was satisfactorily cleaned except for an area around the propeller.

Another significant factor here is that the entire exposed hull shows no significant battle damage. The superficial first time over shows two holes previously mentioned and another hole forward about the size of your fist. The large hole we are expecting to find from battle damage, torpedo damage then must lie under this area that is yet untouched. We are now satisfied with this area at the stern and around the propeller and rudder.

We will now move to the other side of the ship and dig trenches in the following priority, one down the front of the turret, one down the rear of the turret wide enough to include the main hatch, one down across the area of the engine room hatch, this being the largest hatch on the ship, access to the engine room and then one across the hatch to the chain locker forward at frame 21. I would like to report, in all this area that I inspected, the hull and everything that I found seemed to be good. We are going to hold off taking any samples of metal, wood or possible air for another two or three days until we have an initial survey and an evaluation of the integrity of this hull.

I went down to where the dredge head was located on the hole and was right back by the screw just forward of the screw. I took a piece of line 100 feet long and a probing iron and started inspecting the bottom side from the keel up to the armor belt, which would be the side next to the shore, the deepest side and the ship up-right naturally would be the port side. I inspected this area from the keel down to where I could probe through the soft mud and push all the places with a four to five foot iron piece of pipe and hit the armor belt. Some places along the edge still had some large chunks and pieces of log laying there and naturally I could not get past those and we got a narrow trench, probably 4 feet wide that a diver can work in nicely between that and the hull.

Generally since the blow Thursday afternoon, we have been unable to get this operation back on the track. I am sure by tomorrow morning we will have some action and a new set of ground rules as far as this job is concerned. We have now decided that the important thing is to keep this dredge on the job and operating[14]

Day Nine, Sunday, July 16 (CALLAND/MILLER/LAWRENCE)

The bay has calmed down to almost a mirror like surface, no wind and no ripple, absolutely ideal. Tide slackened to practically no movement.

Careful marking of the bow that would then have a permanent and fixed buoy on the shoe at the propeller and one at the bow. About mid day, repairs had been completed on the dredge and they started pumping to clean around the stern so that we could expose the propeller, rudder and the over-hang [sponson; a projection from the side of a ship] *at the rear. This was to allow very careful inspection of this area on the possibility that before maneuvering this ship to right her or raise her would start, that it might be necessary to remove the rudder and propeller to prevent damage. It is necessary, of course, to remove material at both sides of the rudder post and the propeller and the back part of the ship.*

The original Coast Guard buoy, which has been in position all along, was moved up to mark the bow position. It was anchored very carefully on a timber that lies under the bow. We cannot attach the buoy to the ship for there are no mooring devices or any semblance on the forward ram of the ship to attach anything to.

IMPORTANT—In one of the deep holes that have been dredged to the east side of the hull and apparently running under the wreck, we have discovered a railroad iron, although not completely covered here is a railroad iron that lies under the ship. It is surmised and very logically that these are the railroad irons that were probably used to anchor mines (torpedoes) that were placed in the harbor by the Confederate forces.[15]

Day Ten, Monday, July 17 (CALLAND/MILLER/STOKESBERRY)

Miller located the hole right beneath the turret on the starboard side just on the bottom at the starboard side of the keel. The hole is about 2½ plates wide with a definite rupture leading into an area with smaller holes. The dredging is continuing and we will measure more precisely and mark the hole.

IMPORTANT—Primary confirmation at this point of torpedo damage—The dished out area can only be from underwater explosion. While investigating the depressed area, I found a little moon-shaped rupture of about 8 inches long and maybe 2½ inches wide approximately 3 inches from the center of that moon-shape on the outer circumference, I found a round hole 2½–3 inches in diameter. These holes indicated they had been there from time immortal because the corrosion and build-up was the same all over. I circled around to the keel and was able to identify that this depressed area is on the starboard side of the ship and starts approximately at the edge of <u>AA</u> strake [a strake is continuous line of overlapping planks or plates forming the hull], *along the side of the keel. At the <u>B</u> strake, there is a ruptured butt in the plate and then the rupture runs fore and aft on the starboard side of that plate with the rivets busted out. Upon leaving the depressed area and going towards the west or toward the starboard side, I came over the turn of the bilge, down the side of the vessel and was able to find the armor belt. Spent most of afternoon attempting to dredge under the vessel to locate the turret. We are not sure exactly where we are in relation to the turret but we are in front of it and pretty close. The tide is running so that periodic inspections are not too profitable.*[16]

———

Day Eleven, Tuesday, July 18 (CALLAND//MILLER)

Miller will not only go down and get a good survey of the amount of dredging we have completed and estimate what we have to do yet but he will also start checking the hull over in detail and spend a little time around that break and try to get a description of that.

It is obvious in reviewing the operation since we have moved to the west side of the ship, that this ship has rolled over further than we thought. We have her starboard rail is down deeper that we thought it was and is almost as deep as the port rail, so this ship has turned rather than we originally thought maybe 135° to 140°. I would estimate it now about 160° to 165°. We are more upside down than we thought.

IMPORTANT

We now have a tunnel under the bow of the ship that runs down about five feet below, it is narrow and unsafe to use as a diving entry. Miller agrees that the deck is almost 20° certainly not more than 25° off horizontal.

We also believe that because we have to go here that the bow is lower than the stern. First of all, it is because of its length and reach, it is laying a little deeper water but we also think that the whole ship is inclined down at the bow. We already have the stern, propeller and all that completely exposed and ready for detailed examination which is much easier than we were experiencing on the bow.

At 11:20 p.m. final dredging operations are closed down. The official time on the job = 160 hours and 6 minutes for the dredging crew.[17]

Day Twelve, Wednesday, July 19 (STOKESBERRY/CALLAND/B. MILLER/J. MILLER/G. HALL/R.MILLER/P. LADNIER)

The salvage was progressing under the supervision and recommendation of the Supervisor of Salvage of the Navy. We have repositioned the barge after checking the fathometer instrument on the "Suit-Me" and have moved inshore approximately 100 feet and are now anchored with three anchors in position over the wreck. Miller making his first dive of the day but unable to locate the hull so positioned the barge further toward shore. Miller's second dive he located the hull after repositioning the barge according to Colonel Calland's directions.

Miller landed on the hull near the bow and proceeded aft to the damaged area. There he recovered the line that had been previously shackled into the damaged area...he is going to make a dive momentarily to try to attach a buoy on the rudder shoe of the wreck.

Went back to battle damage area and tried to probe a little bit. Found that above the C strake, this plating is busted in two and is blown in leaving room enough that was able to get down in the hole to approximately my waist. While investigating, and moving the mud around by hand I found a bulkhead running fore and aft at approximately the juncture of the C and D strakes. Using a probe, I immediately struck a bulkhead or what I took to be a bulkhead. This bulkhead, being approximately three feet aft of the entry of this hole that I let myself into, pretty well.

IMPORTANT—confirms the location of this battle damage and while doing this I was on the lookout for anything I might find that was solid yet be anything besides a conk or oyster shell. In doing so I found something, I have no idea what it is. Colonel Calland has it and will attempt to identify it.

IMPORTANT—Stokesberry commented on the measurements of the battle damage at the <u>C</u> strake of the starboard hull between frames 91 and 93 which is immediately underneath the turret. This confirms accounts given by survivors of the vessel it also is the size of the hole indicates an instant opening from the explosion and bears on the speed of her sinking.[18]

————

Day Thirteen, Thursday, July 20 (CALLAND/LAWRENCE/ MILLER/STOKESBERRY)

Rain storm!
Miller to begin sample taking from frame <u>B</u> between 91 and 93 as high on the ship as possible. Now the <u>H</u> strake is in partly covered at the top by this sponson. This is also the juncture inside of the ship of the birth deck level. If there is room to get the 12-inch sample there, and to patch it with a 16-inch square without running into complications we will take the sample on the <u>H</u> strake, otherwise we will drop down to <u>G</u> strake. The location of this to keep it as high as possible is that as this ship rolled everything tended to fall away from the starboard of the ship. As she continued to roll, things fell to the center line of the ship and then as she went over to the overhead. It's not likely that anything got back to the starboard side and that would not be jumbled with materials and equipment within the ship.

My main purpose was to inspect on the starboard side from the bow back aft to see how well that was cleared out and also underneath the deck if possible to locate the anchor....I hadn't worked back more than 8 to 12 feet and I ran into a fitting of some sort right on the top of the main deck....I worked around this area: IMPORTANT—I LOCATED THE ANCHOR! It seemed to be 10 feet down in the mud but I believed it was on the ship until the dredge washed out underneath this area, then fell into the hole that was dredged. I can feel the top end of the anchor and a piece of chain coming out this bearing on the deck which seems parted from the anchor itself. Made second dive to get a hold of the anchor with a line. I followed the armor belt back from the anchor back to the turret.

The TURRET IS PULLED AWAY FROM THE HULL further on the centerline there than it was when I originally inspected around the turret.[19]

––––––––

Day Fourteen, Friday, July 21 (STOKESBERRY/CALLAND/B. MILLER)

Weather today is ideal, water is flat and calm. Sky clearing.

Jim Maddox, Engineer, aboard the engineer's survey boat HAZE, with survey crew to take hydrographic soundings over-lay on the same stations on which they took last March or April. Today, divers Buster Miller and Earl Lawrence with George Hall, Paul Ladnier and Jack Diamond as tenders. Local television station, WALA, channel 10 in Mobile will be out to get some coverage today.

We have briefed National Geographic photographer Fred Ward on the geography of the ship and what conditions we have, physical conditions of the ship so he can make a plan to start photography. One thing on the agenda today is to make an entry on the battle damage area. We will

hold that until visibility is the best possible to support photography and will bring up the anchor and get some shots of that.

Miller is making first dive of the day and his objective is to inspect the cleared area of the turret surface and forward along the deck. Earl Lawrence just came up from his first dive of today. Covered the area around the turret trying to find the gun ports and was able to cover an area all the way forward. He believes he covered a third of the surface of the turret but has not been able to locate a gun port. Went up to the bow to try to look under the bow to find the second anchor. This area where the first anchor was pulled yesterday is already filled with logs.

Anchor being raised on July 21, 1967, in preparation to be sent to the Smithsonian Institution in Washington, D.C. *Mobile Press photograph.*

[Note: The anchor was raised on the twenty-first to be photographed. It was lowered back in to the water until the twenty-third.]

We made pictures of dive crew working around the hole which was caused by the torpedo. This is the clearest day I have seen, the close-up photography is extremely good. The second dive of the day was to raise the anchor and there I got some pictures of both Buster and Lawrence working around the anchor, both at the bottom and about 2/3 of the way towards the top where the water is clear and the light is better.

Miller brought up a hull plating sample which looks to be not only good but practically undamaged; both sides smooth, very thick, very grey, and very hard. Back of this wood, it seemed to be a 1x4 timber facing on the inside of the hull. Near the seams of the boards you could run the ice pick in about ½ inch and it was rather spongy but as soon as you got away from the edge of the boards, the ice pick would only go in about ¼ of an inch so it has not been attacked by worms in that area of the coal bunker.[20]

———

Day Fifteen, Saturday, July 22 (CALLAND/WARD/MILLER/ LAWRENCE)

Day for patching holes.

After consultation with National Geographic photographer Fred Ward, who has the responsibility for all news coverage, WALA-TV was allowed permission to take their coverage with the right to preview and refer to the National Geographic before any use was made of that film. The news station was allowed unrestricted photographs of the activity of raising the anchor from a motor launch off shore. The Associated Press arrived and got the necessary coverage for their paper.

4x6 plates of metal will be used to patch the holes. Each plate will be tacked down at the corners of each. This will be a barrier to intrusion by souvenir hunters. Sand bags will be packed around the sides to prevent the intrusion of sand or marine life.

My next concern was for the anchor which had so much publicity. Although weighing 2000 pounds, does not present too great a problem to even the most amateur salvage people. The best thing is to get the thing up and secure above the water. This, of course entails the immediate process of its preservation. The first day, we found the anchor was in the bottom of that where we moved in preparation to raising it which is a good thing because by Friday that area where we found the anchor was completely filled in and the anchor would not have been available to us. When we

Another view of *Tecumseh*'s anchor being raised by a crane aboard the dredge. *Smithsonian Institution, SIA 2020-002843.*

raised the anchor this time, the cross arm had fallen out and this was one of the last things today.

I directed Lawrence to suit up immediately and to go down and find it and not leave it for another minute although the current was bad but that was the very type of thing to be lost in the mud and disappear forever. This was a rather depressing event, however: fortunes be what they may on this job most of which have been good. Earl went down and was able to locate it, got a line on it and brought it up and on board.

This of course further confirms my opinion, once something is found, it must be recovered right then because on this particular anchor we could have lost access to the whole thing and then a second time we could have lost the cross bar. Extreme emphasis has got to be made thorough.

Discovered the hatch to the wardroom, not only discovered it but it was slipped back about 8 inches. The matter of closing battle damage area was discussed with Lawrence stating the requirement that there must be security against any entry and the intrusion of marine life. His first plan [was] to *cover this with large sheet of plywood and weigh it down with sand bags. I informed him that his method was good and of his own choosing but I could not agree that this was secure and requested that he consider some metal and putting over this area and patching this area was much better than sand bags. My feeling was that the sand would wash away and the plywood would float away. He agreed and ordered four 4X6 plates of metal. They will be here Monday.*[21]

———

Day Sixteen, Sunday, July 23 (LAWRENCE/ CALLAND/MILLER)

Final inspection of the hull. Looked around the bow area real good and as it just so happened we have pretty good visibility and I came down the armor belt from the bow to the vicinity of the turret and decided to go underneath the deck and see how fast this was filled in. I also had in the back of my mind to look for a hatch that I supposed to be forward of the turret. On my way under there I did happen to run into a combing [a raised frame around a hatchway in the deck of a ship, to keep water out] *around this hatch. It was almost past the centerline between the center line and the edge of the deck on the opposite side of which we had our entrance dredged underneath which would be the port side of the ship. My indication was that this hatch had been, they* [the crew] *had tried to open it and it had slid forward about 5 inches.*

There was no visibility, so feeling around, I could feel the opening was full of mud but there was an opening so I dug in the mud in this opening which was about 5 inches wide and as I felt and dug I kept hitting something with my hand. I pulled it out and it felt like a dish! I soon found more lying right in this opening and as I dug further inside, picked up about 4 or 5 pieces of dishes, a couple of them were plates and a soup bowl.

Stokesberry, the Smithsonian Institution's representative on board, was especially concerned when I came up, so we took some pictures of these. When I went back down, it was really kind of hairy going back underneath. While standing there, I could feel stuff filling up around my knees. On a second dive, I was able to get 2 or 3 more pieces out and brought them up. The third dive, around 2:30, it was really hard to get under there this time. The thick mud was oozing in and filling around my knees and I could barely work my way through. I got back to the hole and picked up this wheel of affair which Stokesberry said was a ventilator in the lower deck.

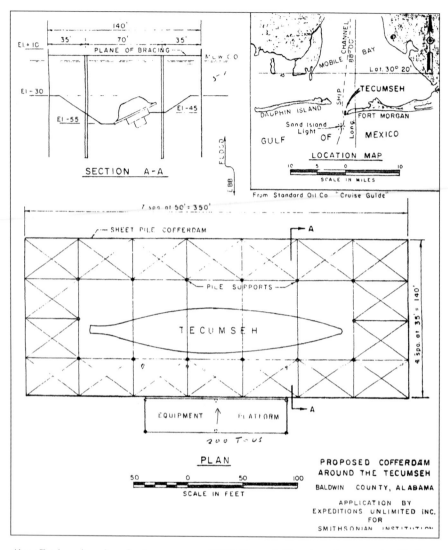

Above: Engineering plans for the recovery of USS *Tecumseh*. Drawing of proposed cofferdam around the *Tecumseh*. *Application by Expeditions Unlimited, Inc. for the Smithsonian Institution.*

Opposite, top: Detail drawing of *Tecumseh* inside cofferdam. *Louis J. Capozzoli & Associates, Inc., consulting engineer.*

Opposite, bottom: Drill platform for light equipment to be used in the operation. *Louis J. Capozzoli & Associates, Inc., Consulting Engineers.*

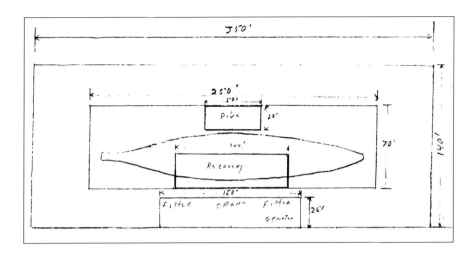

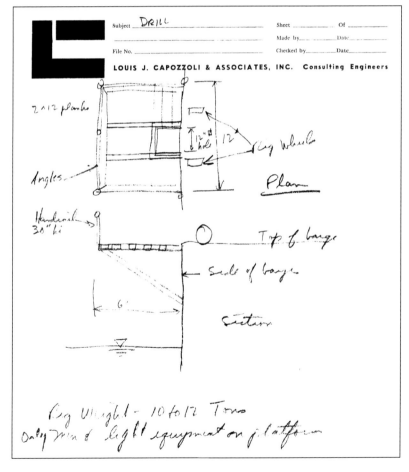

What we have done with these plates and toggle bolts, we have drawn them down real tight, then took a burning torch and burned the toggle bolt itself off right at the nut so the nut will not back off with any type wrench. The only way to get these nuts off is to burn them off. It will take a major operation to get these holes open. This is my last reporting on tape.

Lawrence—I have the samples of the plate that we took out of Tecumseh and it is going to Washington. Tonight we will wrap up this barge and will take the samples and air-freight them to Washington tomorrow about noon. Now that the Mobile Bay part is over, I suggest that as soon as possible the ship systems command people, supervisor of salvage and Smithsonian Institution people get together and have a little confab over this thing. We need a little cooperation when we get back to Washington.[22]

The project was abandoned in 1974 due to lack of funding and the cancellation of plans of Bicentennial Park to be located on five to ten acres in the Washington, D.C. area.

Tecumseh was placed in the National Register of Historic Places by the National Park Service on May 14, 1975 (#75000306) and has been designated a National War Grave.

A typical cellular cofferdam comprises interconnected cells that form a watertight wall. These cells are filled with soils to provide stability against various lateral forces. Such a wall allows the interior of the cofferdam to be dewatered.

9

RECOVERED ARTIFACTS

A report dated February 7, 1976, by Robert M. Organ, chief of the Conservation Analytical Laboratory (CAL), Smithsonian Institution, to the Smithsonian's National Armed Forces Museum Advisory Board, indicates that "the conclusion was reached that it would not be possible with the preservation materials and methods available at the present time to treat the raised ship with all of its materials in situ." This is based on a shortage of qualified conservators and the impracticability of treatment when the vessel is out of the water. He suggested that the only practical way is by using a cofferdam. The report concludes with a recommendation that a supervising conservator be present throughout the entire process. The artifact count is estimated to be 50,000.[1]

On November 25, 1968, Smithsonian historian James J. Stokesberry released his twenty-one-page CAL report containing general information on *Tecumseh*, including the objectives consisting of reviewing the existing methods of treating wood and iron. The report also includes vessel measurements and materials believed to be specified used in *Tecumseh's* construction, such as wrought iron, wooden deck beams, bronze in engines and zinc paint on the hull. "The main objective was to recommend procedures, based upon samples submitted for the preservation of the raised ship. These involve the problem of treatment of a very large object constructed of dissimilar materials, which are in contact with one another, using treatments which are both compatible with one another and if possible reversible."[2]

Top, left: Eighteen-inch engine room signal gong recovered in 1967. *Hampton Roads Naval Museum, Norfolk, Virginia.*

Top, right: Eight-and-one-quarter-inch-diameter ironstone dinnerware from wardroom area. *Navy Memorial Museum, Washington Navy Yard, Washington, D.C.*

Right, middle: Ten-and-one-quarter-by-three-and-three-fourths-inch ironstone tureen dinnerware from wardroom area. *Navy Memorial Museum, Washington Navy Yard, Washington, D.C.*

Right, bottom: Confederate anvil recovered from Fort Powell during a 1978 expedition to the site. The author donated the anvil to the History Museum of Mobile. *Alabama Gulf Coast Archaeological Society Inc.*

Bottom, left: Four-inch-high, three-inch-wide glass tumbler from wardroom area, *Navy Memorial Museum, Washington Navy Yard, Washington, D.C.*

Top, left: Nine-and-one-quarter-inch-diameter ironstone dinnerware from wardroom area. *Hampton Roads Naval Museum, Norfolk, Virginia.*

Top, right: Ironstone dinnerware. *L 2004 .2 .2, Hampton Roads Naval Museum, Norfolk, Virginia.*

Bottom, left: Dinner plate with manufacturer's stamp on the bottom. *Hampton Roads Naval Museum, Norfolk, Virginia.*

Bottom, right: Two three-by-two-inch and one two-by-two-inch wrought-iron steering chain links. *Fort Morgan Historic Site, Mobile Point, Alabama.*

Above: *Tecumseh*'s nine-by-four-foot Trotman anchor displayed after its arrival in Washington. *Naval Historical Center, Washington Navy Yard, Washington, D.C.*

Left: Ten-by-seven-inch iron and lignum vita pulley. *Naval Historical Center, Washington Navy Yard, Washington, D.C.*

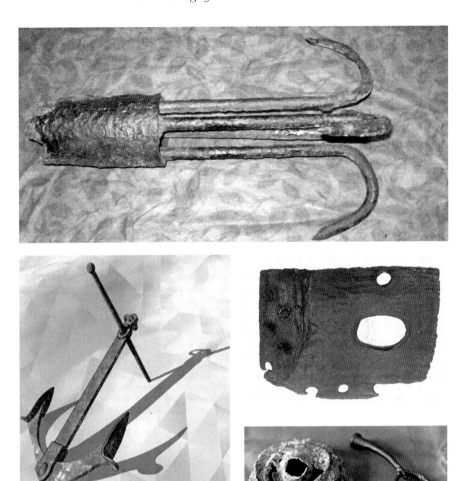

Top: Union navy grapple recovered from upper Mobile Bay obstructions during 1978 expedition. The author donated the grapple to the History Museum of Mobile. *Alabama Gulf Coast Archaeological Society Inc.*

Right, middle: Section of iron hull. Wrought-iron plate from torpedo-damaged area measuring thirteen and one half-by ten inches. *History Museum of Mobile, Alabama.*

Right, bottom: Five-inch diameter candleholder base and six-inch stem, *Naval Historical Center, Washington Navy Yard, Washington, D.C.*

Left: Trotman anchor modeled after anchor from *Tecumseh*. Mobile Press *photo*.

10

SUBSEQUENT SURVEYS

Since the two week inspection of Tecumseh, July 7 to July 23, 1967, by the Smithsonian's "Tecumseh Project," there have been nine officially sanctioned surveys of Tecumseh . The Smithsonian project had the greatest impact on the site and yielded the single largest body of data that we have on the wreck today.[1]

1864

November 9, Mr. T.H. Bacon from Boston requested permission to salvage *Tecumseh*, but Secretary of the Navy Wells refused his request on November 15.

1873

"August 3, 1873, James E. slaughter of Mobile purchased salvage rights to the *Tecumseh* from the Department of the Treasury for fifty dollars."[2]

"After the purchase, Slaughter let it be known that he intended to use explosives to blast the wreck into salvageable pieces in order to recover the iron and possibly the ship's safe. The news of his plans provoked relatives of the men lost on the *Tecumseh* to petition Congress in 1876 to stop the salvage. Reacting quickly to the requests Congress passed a joint resolution on August 15, 1876, directing the Secretary of the Treasury to 'return and tender to the party claiming to have purchased the United States monitor *Tecumseh* the sum of fifty dollars, with interest at six per centum'.[3] The act further empowered the Secretary of the Navy to 'assume the control and protection of said monitor' and authorize him to dispose of the wreck, 'providing in such disposition for the removal from said monitor and the proper burial of the remains of the persons carried down when she sunk.'"[4]

1965

An unknown group became interested in salvaging *Tecumseh* and placing it on exhibit in Mobile, Alabama, along with artifacts from the ship. *Tecumseh* could be legally sold by the General Services Administration to qualified salvagers, provided "the removal and burial of the crew" be part of the agreement; however, the director of naval history was concerned that the salvors may not be qualified, which would lead to the "the destruction and indiscriminant piecemeal disposition of artifacts."

The same year, the Smithsonian Institution expressed an interest in conducting its own salvage and restoration project.

1968

"In March 1968, Norman Scott, Vice President of Expeditions Unlimited, Inc. (EUI) of Pompano Beach, Florida, approached Colonel (John H.) Magruder with an offer to salvage *Tecumseh*. He proposed to raise the ironclad 'at a cost of $1.00 to the Smithsonian Institution' with certain conditions. EUI would be the general contractor for the project and would have rights to the salvage. Also, EUI would have 'exclusive motion picture, TV, newspaper, literary and commercial rights,' for the vessel and the project. Scott submitted a preliminary salvage plan and budget to Colonel Magruder on June 18. Colonel Magruder informed Scott that Captain W.F. Searle Jr. would review EUI's Proposal and give his opinion as to its feasibility. Magruder agreed that an exploratory dive should be made as soon as possible."[5]

"EUI conducted a reconnaissance survey the week of July 14, 1968. The divers noted that the deck and turret chamber beams had been completely destroyed by shipworms (teredo navalis). The survey was completed on August 1 and the plate was resecured over the battle-damaged area. December 13, EUI, Murphy-Pacific and Palmer-Baker presented their salvage plan to the Smithsonian project team."[6]

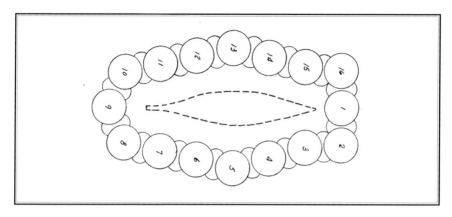

Conceptual drawing of a cellular-wall cofferdam for the EUI recovery project. *Palmer-Baker Engineering Inc.*

1969

After many meetings and the financial report presentation, the Smithsonian met with board members in Washington, D.C., on June 4 to discuss the project and declared that EUI would not have sufficient funds to begin Phase One by the July 1, 1969 deadline. "With adequate funding unavailable and the chances of postponement unlikely, EUI had no alternative but to withdraw. On June 26, James Bradley, Acting Secretary of the Smithsonian, withdrew the letter of intent."[7]

1975

May 15, 1975, *Tecumseh* was placed in the National Register of Historic Places. "In a letter to E. Joseph Wheeler on August 12, 1975, the General Services Administration stated they did not believe that 'the best interest of the United States, in preserving *Tecumseh* would be served by awarding a contract to a state that was unwilling to accept any responsibility with respect to the project.' This impasse could not be resolved and the Bicentennial passed with *Tecumseh* still miffed in mud and controversy."[8]

1977–78

On October 15, 1977, the (Alabama) Gulf Coast Archaeological Society Inc. searched an area 267 yards west of Mobile Point in the mouth of Mobile Bay. A 120 Dolfin Flashed fathometer was used to determine that the depth of the search area was twenty-five to twenty-nine feet deep. "During the dive, visibility was six feet at four feet above bottom and zero at the bottom."[9]

The purpose of the survey was to plot the position of the vessel and determine the condition of the hull, which was now exposed. The project also served as a training exercise for the divers who are involved in the underwater archaeological programs of the society.

William R. Armistead, project coordinator, and Sidney H. Schell, project director and dive master, used a Discover IV magnetometer prior to the dive to determine the actual location of *Tecumseh*. Six divers participated in the initial search and were placed equally along a line until they came into contact with the exposed hull area, which was found to be in poor condition. Due to the inability to efficiently plot the location of *Tecumseh* onto a map, an additional survey was conducted on March 19, 1978, and the position was successfully plotted on the Geological Survey map. No artifacts were recovered during the survey, and no features other than the exposed area of the *Tecumseh*'s hull were discovered.

"When the Smithsonian Institution dredged the area around the vessel, a great disservice was done to the vessel by not backfilling and completely covering the hull. The resulting conditions discovered in this survey shows that the hull is rapidly deteriorating. The iron plate is void of any marine growth and the dredged area is filled with soft mud, which shows that the hull was, and is, exposed to rapid current and is corroding at an ever increasing rate."[10]

1985

At the request of the U.S. Army Corps of Engineers, Mobile District, archaeologists with Espy, Huston & Associates (EHA) of Austin, Texas, conducted a cursory examination of *Tecumseh* prior to widening the Mobile ship channel. "The divers found the same area of the turn of the bilge [the part of the hull between the keel and vertical sides] exposed and, although no measurements were taken during the survey, the size was considerably smaller than that reported during the GCAS survey. Three holes were discovered in the hull, two less than six inches, the third was fourteen inches

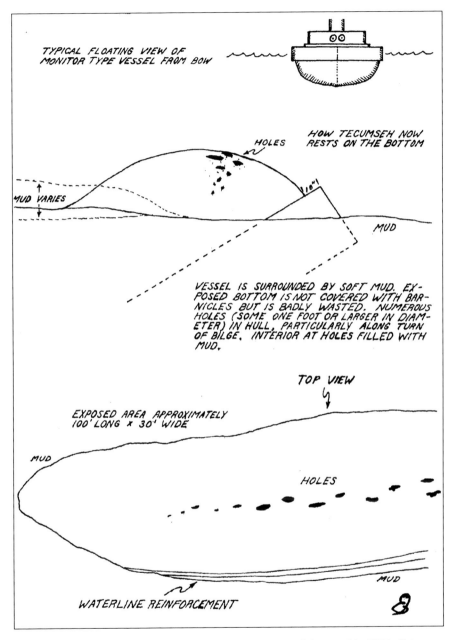

TYPICAL FLOATING VIEW OF
MONITOR TYPE VESSEL FROM BOW

HOW TECUMSEH NOW
RESTS ON THE BOTTOM

HOLES

MUD VARIES

MUD

VESSEL IS SURROUNDED BY SOFT MUD. EX-
POSED BOTTOM IS NOT COVERED WITH BAR-
NICLES BUT IS BADLY WASTED. NUMEROUS
HOLES (SOME ONE FOOT OR LARGER IN DIAM-
ETER) IN HULL, PARTICULARLY ALONG TURN
OF BILGE. INTERIOR AT HOLES FILLED WITH
MUD.

TOP VIEW

EXPOSED AREA APPROXIMATELY
100' LONG x 30' WIDE

MUD

HOLES

MUD

WATERLINE REINFORCEMENT

Detailed drawing of *Tecumseh* position and the exposed area of the vessel in 1977. *Alabama Gulf Coast Archaeological Society Inc. survey.*

wide by twenty inches high and appeared to have been cut with a torch. A rebar, with a line attached, was wedged in the hole. This line ran out of the hole and along the hull. The divers followed this line for several yards before it disappeared into the bottom. They estimated about three feet of sediment over the hull in this area. They found a blue plastic bag and below that the corner of what was described as a 'rubber mat'. The rest of the mat lay under the sediment.

"Their video tape indicated that the holes lie in a line along the hull covering twenty to thirty feet. If the compartments exposed by this entry were clear or lightly silted, they have since filled with sand and debris. The lack of concretion along the edge of the hole, and excellent condition of the lines, indicates the intrusion was recent."[11]

This survey revealed the most conclusive evidence of unauthorized site disturbance to date. There is no way to determine the period of the infringement when the large cut was made in *Tecumseh*'s hull; the condition of the hole, rebar and lines and the nonappearance in the 1977 Gulf Coast Archaeological Society's site report indicate that it occurred after their survey. Note: The Smithsonian divers bolted closure plates over the numerous holes in the hull, including those cut for samples. As a protective buffer, one-fourth-inch rubber pads or gaskets were placed between the hull and the plates. "The discovery of the torch-cut hole in the hull succeeded in raising the awareness of federal, state and local officials to the many threats to the site, both man-made and natural. In terms of preservation, we are perhaps fortunate that she capsized while sinking, as this low profile aided the subsequent burying process.[12]

1991

"In the summer of 1991, Rod Farb, a commercial underwater photographer, and founder of Farb Monitor Expedition, applied for and received a permit from the NHC to conduct a no disturbance survey of the *Tecumseh* site. Once again, the hull, along the turn of the bilge, was exposed. This time the exposed area measured nearly seventy feet by ten feet. Farb described the wreck as covered with a thin layer of sand over a deep layer of mud. He reported three holes cut into the hull…these holes were described as 'irregular squares…cut with welding rods,' approximately one foot in diameter. Farb also found a rebar and lines in one hole identical to that reported during the 1985 survey, although the sizes of the holes do not correspond. All the openings were filled with sediment. A brief report on the expedition was filed with the Naval Historical Center."[13]

1993

"On October 4, 1993, archaeologists from East Carolina University's Program in Maritime History and Underwater Archaeology conducted the most recent investigation of the site. Funded by the National Park Service's American Battlefield Protection Program, the SCU conducted a Phase I survey of the remains of three participants of the battle of Mobile Bay: *Tecumseh*, USS *Philippi* and CSS *Gaines*. This survey found *Tecumseh* in the same condition as reported by earlier surveys, including low visibility, strong currents and several holes along the exposed turn of the bilge. The large torch-cut hole with rebar and lines was located and drawn. Early in the survey the exposed area measured approximately eight to ten feet long. After two days of strong northeasterly winds, the divers reported this area had enlarged to approximately sixty feet. Two additional small holes were found sixty feet northwest of the large hole in this newly exposed area. The archaeologists believed these were also torch-cut, and all the openings were filled with sediment. As with previous expeditions, the iron hull was reported to be in very good condition. The exposed area was covered by a calcareous crust and only nominal surface deterioration was present. They reported only superficial marine fouling that suggested that this area is not always exposed to the water column."[14]

The East Carolina University team also documented the *Tecumseh*, *Philippi* and *Gaines* sites for the U.S. Department of Interior, National Park Service and U.S. Navy, as an aspect of the study is to recognize Mobile Bay as a battlefield. "The assessment of the wrecks in Mobile Bay may signal some changes in the way the Park Service's battlefield protection program is conducted. The work could lead to protection and management plans for historic nautical battle sites at Mobile Bay."[15]

The National Park Service does periodic surveys to monitor it. Technically, it is still a military vessel. So, although embedded in state water bottoms, it remains federal property. The Alabama state archaeologist with the Alabama Historical Society monitors the vessel's condition. The latest survey showed that it was covered completely in sediment. As of 2019, the survey showed no recent damage.[16]

11

OTHER SALVAGE ATTEMPTS

USS *HARTFORD*

Farragut's flagship USS *Hartford* was launched on November 22, 1858, and was among the last of the wooden hull warships, due to the advent of iron armored vessels and heavier guns, making the wood-hulled warship obsolete. It became Farragut's flagship in 1862. Its assignment was to take the fleet up the Mississippi River and force the surrender of Fort Jackson, Fort St. Phillip and the city of New Orleans. After the fall of New Orleans, Farragut took the fleet into Mobile Bay in 1864 and after the engagement forced the closing of Mobile Bay.

On October 19, 1945, the *Hartford* was towed from Washington, D.C., to the Norfolk Navy Yard on the Elizabeth River and classified as a relic. It was beyond salvage but moored at a pier. After ninety-eight years, it finally succumbed to its age. On November 20, 1957, according to an international News Service Dispatch, "a security patrol noticed early this morning that the old vessel had settled slightly. Fire pumps were unable to empty the vessel and it sank to the bottom in 20 to 25 feet of water several hours later."[1]

The following relics from the *Hartford* were placed on display at Fort Gaines on Dauphin Island: one of its three 9,000-pound anchors and the fifty-foot anchor chain weighing 1,800 pounds. *Hartford*'s steering wheel and stanchion (support), a porthole frame, a bronze cleat (a metal fitting with arms or horns on which secure ship's lines), a brass deck plate, a coal passing scuttle plate

Farragut's wooden-hull flagship USS *Hartford* was launched on November 22, 1858. It carried Farragut through the gauntlet at Mobile Bay on August 5, 1964. On October 19, 1945, *Hartford* was towed to Norfolk Navy Yard. *Naval Shipyard Historical Museum.*

and a wooden bull's eye, as well as photographs of ships that fought in the Battle of Mobile Bay. According to the museum director, unfortunately, the only items that remain at Fort Gaines today from the *Hartford* collection are the anchor and chain. The other items were apparently stolen when the Dauphin Island bridge was destroyed by Hurricane Frederick and the only assess to the island was by boat or aircraft.

Two other articles of great historical interest and value are an eagle and wardroom sideboard removed from the *Hartford* for preservation in the Naval Ship Yard's Historical Museum. The eagle was an original decoration on the fantail, and the sideboard was originally used in the commissioned officers' mess of the famous vessel. Assistant Secretary of the Navy Thomas S. Gates, in a letter to Congress, said, "Salvage of the ship is not feasible."

CSS *MUSCOGEE*/CSS *JACKSON*

Now housed in the National Civil War Naval Museum in Columbus, Georgia, on the banks of the Chattahoochee River, the *Jackson* was commissioned and launched in December 1862. It was initially known as the *Muscogee*, but the name was changed to the *Jackson* when launched. The Columbus Naval Iron

The CSS *Muscogee*/SS *Jackson*, circa mid-1960s. The National Civil War Naval Museum in Columbus, Georgia, is the final resting place for this hulk of charred timbers. *Courtesy of U.S. Naval Historical Center NH 45769.*

Works supplied its machinery but suffered delays in its construction due lack of available iron plating.

The *Jackson* returned to Columbus after river trials in April 1865 to be completed. It was still incomplete when, on April 16, the Battle of Columbus caused its crew to set it on fire and scuttle it as Brigadier General James H. Wilson led his Union Army Calvary Corps forces into Georgia.

In the 1960s, *Jackson*'s remains were discovered. It was raised, and its remains are exhibited at the museum in Columbus. Today, the flat bottom of the ironclad, as well as the fantail, can be viewed from a platform. Although there is a section missing, one can still appreciate its enormous size. It was 222 feet long and 57 feet wide. Strangely, one can still detect the odor of the longleaf pine used on the inner hull.

USS *CAIRO*

The USS *Cairo* is the best-known case of the Civil War ironclad salvage attempts of the 1960s. An attempt to raise it resulted in disaster. In the attempt, cables cut into the hull amidships and severed the stern due to the weight of the vessel. Hundreds of artifacts and the stern section spilled into the river and were lost.

Serving for only eleven months, the *Cairo* had the unfortunate honor of being the first U.S. warship to be sunk by a torpedo (mine) in the Civil War. On December 12, 1862, while on the Yazoo River north of Vicksburg,

Mississippi, the *Cairo* was steaming north when, suddenly, two Confederate torpedoes exploded under it. Within two minutes, it sank in six fathoms of water and settled on the muddy bottom of the river. Fortunately, there was no loss of life of its crew.

Cairo's third commanding officer, Lieutenant Commander Thomas Oliver Selfridge Jr., was an ambitious and demanding young officer who was commanded to clear mines from the Yazoo River to prepare for the attack on Vicksburg. An ensign in a ship's boat found a line in the water that he believed was a lanyard attached to a torpedo and severed it. To his surprise, a mine bobbed to the surface. He discovered another line and was ordered to repeat the process. However, the ensign instead pulled the line to shore, but it did not explode. At almost the same time, an explosion was heard, and as the ensign turned around, he saw *Cairo*'s anchor flying through the air. The vessel had drifted over two of Confederate major general Dabney Maury's powder-filled glass demijohn torpedoes ignited by a cannon fuse (friction primer) when the lanyards were pulled.

Cairo mounted fourteen guns, had a draft of six feet, a crew of 251 and an estimated speed of six to nine knots. It was built by James Eads and Company, Mound City, Illinois, and commissioned on January 28, 1862.

The USS *Cairo* is seen here in its glory days just before being destroyed while on the Yazoo River by two torpedoes. In 1965, efforts to remove it from the river damaged it beyond possibility of salvaging the vessel. *Edwin C. Bearss, National Park Service.*

Three years prior to Smithsonian's discovery of *Tecumseh*, *Cairo* was located by a team headed by a research historian with the National Park Service, Edwin C. Bearss. Its "hard luck" continued, with disastrous results.

Fully intact when located, it was destroyed during the recovery process by being pulled apart and cut into three pieces as well as having the pilothouse destroyed by a crane attempting to pull it off the deck.

In 1965, what was left of the ship was sent to Ingalls Shipyard in Pascagoula, Mississippi, where it languished for years. Twelve years later, in 1977, contracts were awarded to locate the *Cairo* and construct the visitors' center, parking facilities, walkways and utilities at the new facility in Vicksburg.

CSS GEORGIA

In 1980, under a contract with the U.S. Army Corps of Engineers, Texas A&M University surveyed the *Georgia* to lay the groundwork for future exploration. In 1986, approximately one hundred cannonballs, rifled Brooke shells and two cannons were found. They are now on display at Georgia's oldest fort, Old Fort Jackson, located on the Savannah River.

With only a limited amount of factual data on the *Georgia* available to researchers, underwater archaeologists began their daily dives in January 2015. There are no known actual blueprints, only lithographs from newspapers of the period. In 1862, the Ladies Gunboat Association raised close to $120,000 for the building of the vessel, including the railroad iron plates on the casemates to protect it from shelling damage.

It served two years without firing a shot. When Georgia was invaded by Union general William T. Sherman as his army advanced on Savannah in December 1864, it was scuttled by Confederate troops. Archaeologists have recovered over 1,500 artifacts, such as bayonets, accoutrements related to six cannon, numerous cannonballs, grapeshot stands and other similar pieces.

After 150 years of river traffic, dredging of the area and the worst enemy of all for a sunken wooden vessel—teredo worms—severe damage resulted. Although many man-hours and dollars were spent on the project, there are more questions than answers. For now, it still lies at rest in its watery grave.

On Sunday, January 21, 1979, the *Atlanta Journal-Constitution* claimed, "'Seagoing Tank' May Rise Again." It noted that the *Georgia* could be the only salvageable ironclad; however, the statement was made before the discovery

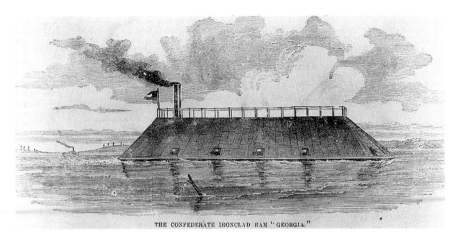

THE CONFEDERATE IRONCLAD RAM "GEORGIA."

In 1980, the U.S. Army Corps of Engineers let a contract to Texas A&M University to survey the CSS *Georgia* to determine the feasibility of raising the vessel. The *Atlanta Journal-Constitution* claimed it may rise again. *U.S. Naval Historical Center Photograph Collection, NH 58722.*

of two Confederate ironclads, the CSS *Huntsville* and CSS *Tuscaloosa*, were located and identified in the Mobile River in 1985.

"Although historians continue to debate the contributions of the monitor to the development of the ocean-going warship, one outstanding feature remains today; the revolving gun turret."[2] The Monitor-class vessels were not very seaworthy due to their design and were assigned coastal operations. Coastal defense training was still used until the twentieth century.

Fifty-one monitors were built during the war, but only nineteen of the Passaic and Canonicus class represent features of the monitor design developed by navy engineers. The vast majority of monitors were decommissioned and scrapped by the end of the nineteenth century. The sinking of *Tecumseh* is the principal reason why it survives today, which is significant, due to its preservation. It may be the most important Civil War relic in the United States.

Today, there are only four surviving U.S. ironclads of Ericsson's design in the world: "the original USS *Monitor*, capsized and deteriorated in 225 feet of water off Cape Hatteras, North Carolina, USS *Weehawken*, of the *Passaic* class, just off shore of Morris Island, South Carolina at the entrance to Charleston Harbor. She was lost in a freak accident in December 1863. In 1871 the Corps of Engineers after extensive channel clearance demolition, reported that the pilothouse, turret and deck were blasted to a depth of eleven and a half feet. The remains of *Weehawken's* hull lies under eight to ten feet of sand. Another *Passaic* class monitor, the USS *Patapsco,* struck a torpedo in the shallow waters of Charleston Harbor, off Fort Sumter in January 1865 with the loss of sixty four officers and men. Efforts to clear her from the channel were also made in 1871. The pilothouse was removed and her turret was inclined 35°. The decks were blown off over the engine room but the engines remained. She remains covered by 15 feet of water. Of the four wrecks mentioned above, *Tecumseh* is the best preserved."[3]

Summary and Conclusions

F actors such as research, location, recovery, relic preservation, underwater technology and experts from many fields all add up to millions of dollars required to implement these projects. In my opinion, lack of funding is the reason most of them fail.

Tecumseh is in the National Register of Historic Places as a war grave. It contains the remains of the ninety-three crew who gave their all. Today, many state and federal laws protect historical sites, abandoned shipwrecks and other antiquities both in the United States and abroad.

Antiquities Act (16 U.S.C. 433)

National Historic Preservation Act of 1966, as amended (16 U.S.C. 470)

Archaeological and Historic Preservation Act of 1974 (16 U.S.C. 469)

Archaeological Resources Protection Act of 1979 (16 U.S.C. 470AA)

Theft of Government Property (18 U.S.C. 641)

Abandoned Shipwreck Act of 1987 (43 U.S.C. 2101)

Documents, Historical Artifacts and Condemned or Obsolete Combat Material: Loan, Gift, or Exchange (10 U.S.C. 2572)

Archaeological Resources Protection Act, Final Uniform Regulations (32 U.S.C. 229)

Protection of Historic Properties (36 CFR 229)

Secretary of the Interior's Standards of Historic Preservation Projects (36 CFR 800)

Abandoned Shipwreck Act Guidelines (55 CFR 50116)

National Register of Historic Places (36 CFR 60)

Determinations of Eligibility for Inclusion in the National Register of Historic Places (36 CFR 63)

Underwater Cultural Resources Chapter 460-X-12, Alabama Historical Commission

Alabama Submerged Historical Cultural Resources Act

Abandonment in the maritime salvage context has been defined as the "act of leaving or deserting such property by those who were in charge of it, without hope on their part of recovering it and without the intention of returning to it." The United States owns all sunken military vessels anywhere in the world they may be.

"Over the last few years the Naval Historical Center has dealt with many policy issues involving U.S. Navy ship and aircraft wrecks and other government-owned wrecks that are entitled to sovereign immunity."

The Department of the Navy retains custody of its ship and aircraft wrecks despite the passage of time and regardless of whether they are lost in U.S., foreign or international waters. These wrecks are not abandoned but remain the property of the government until a specific formal action is taken to dispose of them and, thus, are immune from the law of salvage without authorization from the appropriate navy authorities. (Abandoned Shipwreck Act of 1987, 43 U.S.C. 2101-2106)."[1]

Tecumseh is considered the best-preserved Civil War monitor in existence. The ship is completely intact and contains an estimated 50,000 artifacts.[2]

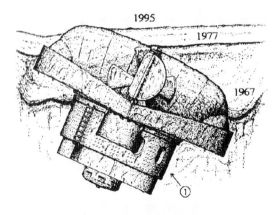

1995

1977

1967

Stern (list = approximately 155°)

USS *Tecumseh* depth chart showing a stern view of *Tecumseh* upside down at 155 degrees, 1967, 1977, 1995. *National Park Service.*

Appendix A

List of officers of U.S. ironclad *Tecumseh*, corrected up to July 5, 1864

Name[1]	Rank
T.A. Craven	Commander
J.W. Kelley	Lieutenant
John Faron	Chief Engineer
George Work	Acting Assistant Paymaster
H.A. Danker	Acting Assistant Surgeon
C.F. Langley	Acting Master
Gardner Cottrell	ditto
J.P Zettick	ditto
Charles W. Pennington	Acting First Assistant Engineer
W.L. Pennell	ditto
H.B. Green	Acting Second Assistant Engineer
F. Scott	Acting Third Assistant Engineer
William D. Kay	ditto
Josiah Conly	Captain's Clerk
Jacob Vreeland	Yeoman
Thomas Burges	Paymaster's Steward

Robert Price[*]   Acting Ensign
H.S. Leonard[†]   Second Assistant Engineer
Thomas Ustick[‡]   Acting Second Assistant Engineer
Webster Lane[§]   Second Assistant Engineer

[*] Transferred from the tug *Rose*, June 8, 1864
[†] Transferred from the tug *Roanoke*, June 18, 1864
[‡] Transferred from the tug *Minnesota*, June 18, 1864
[§] Transferred from the tug *Roanoke*, June 1, 1864; transferred at Port Royal
    to another vessel.

LIST OF MEN TRANSFERRED TO THE USS *TECUMSEH* FROM THE RECEIVING SHIP *NORTH CAROLINA*, APRIL 1864

Allison, Samuel M.
Barry, Ambrose M.
Barry, Thomas C.
Bartholomew, H.L.
Bell, John
Berry, John Burnett, Robert
Blades, James
Blagher, John
Brady, William
Brown, John L.
Burns, Edward
Burns, Jacob
Callahan, Patrick E.
Campbell, Barney
Chapman, George
Christie, James
Churchill, William J.
Collins, Richard
Collins, Richard T.
Conolly, Peter
Cousins, Edward
Cousins, Frank

Cowan, Robert
Cullen, James
Dalton, James L.
Davis, Thomas
Dean, Chauncey P.
Deans, Robert
Delano, Nathaniel B.
Derris, Charles C.
Duval, James
Evans, Charles
Finn, James
Fletcher, Henry
Foster, Fred
Francis, Charles
Gould, John
Grady, John J.
Hamilton, William
Hannible, Charles
Harwood, Robert H.
Hatch, Charles A.[***]
Haverty, Benjamin
Heisler, Joseph

Hogan, Patrick	Multoy, James
Holland, Alfred	O'Brien, Nicholas
Horan, William	O'Wston, James C.
Hurley, Jeremiah	Packard, Charles A.
Jay, John	Parker, Peter E.
Johnson, William	Pemberton, Charles J.
Kane, James	Powers, Walter
Kearn, James	Rayner, James
Kennedy, James	Roberts, William
Kindler, James	Smith, James
Kostix, John	Thom, James
Lawless, James	Walker, Edward
Lesk, Thomas	West, William C.
Lyman, Gilbert A.	Williams, David
Matts, George	Williams, John
McAllister, James	Wilson, John
McCue, James	Wooley, George A.
McDonald, James	Worth, Jacob H.
McEllery, Michael	Wrenn, John

***Charles Able Hatch, Ordinary Seaman

An interesting letter concerning Charles A. Hatch is related here. In March 1967, when I was on the *Tecumseh* committee of the Mobile Junior Chamber of Commerce, I received a three-page letter from Emily "Fifi" Hosmer of Covington, Louisiana, concerning her relative Charles Able Hatch, who was listed in the *Official Record* (Series I, Volume 21, page 492) as an ordinary seaman serving on the *Tecumseh* when it sank.

Seaman Hatch was born in Castine, Maine, on August 14, 1843. Mrs. Hosmer continued in her letter relating the family history and asking that, if the ship is raised, the remains of these men be interred together in a dignified manner.[2]

Appendix B

Engineers, Shipbuilders, Ironworks, Rolling Mills

History has a way of producing the right people at the right time.[1] The American Civil War was no exception. Neither the North nor the South was prepared for a four-year war that would need a mass navy using mass guns aboard mass iron warships. At the opening of the war, the North had 42 ships; at the conclusion, 671. The South began with none. Listed here are several mills that produced these incredible machines of war.

When iron ships of the period are discussed, the Swedish-born inventor and engineer John Ericsson is at the top of the list of relevant people, with his ingenious mind and the recognition of his capabilities by the right people. An example of his work was his "caloric engine." He used heated exhaust combined with fresh air and used a cylinder that could transfer heated exhaust air to be compressed in the working cylinder of the engine. This transfer of air took place in a wire-meshed box called a "regenerator." For additional heat, he placed a small firebox below the working cylinder. The result was a hot-air engine. Ericsson built the first caloric ship, *Ericsson*. It was a large steamship with caloric engines operating its paddle wheels. It was 260 feet long with a 40-foot beam and was launched in September 1862. *Scientific American* reported: "Captain Ericsson is a very skillful, scientific and ingenious engineer." The *New York Tribune*: "Ericsson is the greatest mechanical genius of the present and the future." On January 19, 1860, the *New York Times* reported: "This motor may be confidently pronounced one of the greatest boons which the ingenuity of man has ever bestowed upon his race."[2]

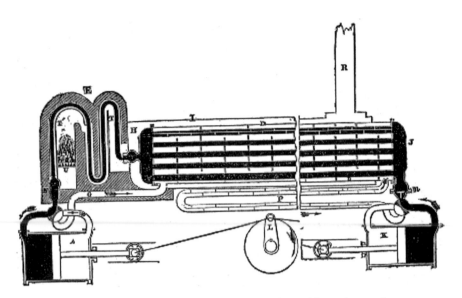

Ericsson's caloric engine. Mechanic's Magazine and Register of Inventions and Improvements *III (February 1834): 65.*

MAJOR IRON MANUFACTURERS

Perhaps the most famous ironclad vessels of the Civil War naval battles were the USS *Monitor* and CSS *Virginia.* I chose to concentrate on the *Monitor* because of the vast number of mechanics, engineers and inventors it took to produce the technological changes from wooden warships to iron ones. A major factor in the development of rolling mills was the fast advancement of the railroad industry. In 1860, there were 256 ironworks in twenty states producing railroad iron, bars and sheets of iron; over one-half of the iron ore came from Pennsylvania, Ohio and New York.

Located on the western edge of Rensselaer County, on the eastern bank of the Hudson River, Troy, New York contained eight blast furnaces, twenty forges, three rolling mills and two foundries at the beginning of the Civil War. The Albany Ironworks as well as the Rensselaer Ironworks produced the iron for the USS *Monitor.* Holdane & Company in New York City produced boiler and sheet iron, rivets and welding tubes and provided 125 tons of armor plating, angle iron and bar. The war saw Albany Ironworks expand to forty or fifty acres and consisting of many buildings and over 750 employees.[3]

Another Troy mill was the Rensselaer Ironworks, a converted rolling mill formally known as Troy Vulcan Company consisting of eighteen furnaces and four steam-driven roll trains producing 12,600 tons of rail and 862 tons of bar iron. With 350 employees, the ironworks manufactured railroad rails, bar and sheet iron. At the beginning of the war, both the Albany and Rensselaer ironworks employed over 1,000 men.[4]

Niagara Steam Forge was located in Buffalo and manufactured "port stoppers." (When the turret guns were not in use or withdrawn for reloading during battle, heavy iron port stoppers would swing down to close the gun ports.) It also produced railroad car axles, crank axles, track cranks, connecting rods, driving axles, wrought-iron driving wheels, locomotive frames, steamboat propeller shafts, piston rods, crank pins, mill shafts, anchors, bar iron and blacksmithing.[5]

F.H. Abbott & Sons of Baltimore, Maryland, and Niagara Steam Forge both produced armor plate for the turret of the USS *Monitor*. By 1861, Horace Abbott had expanded to three mills.[6]

In 1861, *Scientific American* reported that the New York City steam-engine manufacturing firms were very busy. Novelty Ironworks and Delamater Ironworks were working on building the *Monitor*'s turret. Novelty became one of the largest companies in the United States for building marine engines. The ironworks also manufactured more than seventy-five steam-fire engines designed by Lee & Larned as well as two iron vessels for the government, as well as a surveying steamer and a cutter for the Revenue Cutter Service.[7]

MAJOR MACHINERY MANUFACTURERS

In the prior decade, Novelty Ironworks Foundry occupied nearly one thousand yards along the East River and included four furnaces, a blacksmith's shop and other buildings and employed 1,170 people. There were also two slips capable of docking eight to ten large vessels. A visitor to the foundry wrote, "I found an immense establishment in which were carried on all the different branches and operations in any way connected with making stoves, steam engines, boilers, and almost every article of large machinery and even steamboats."

Eliphalet Knott, the founder of Novelty, was an "energetic and unremitting inventor." He named his foundry Novelty because he had constructed a steamboat that he named *Novelty*, the first to be fueled by anthracite coal, a highly carbonated form of clean-burning coal that is different from the more commonly known bituminous or soft coal. In other words, it is smokeless. This type of coal was used in *Tecumseh*.[8]

Perhaps the most profitable of the machinery manufacturers was Delamater Ironworks in New York City, which built most of *Monitor's* machinery. It is no surprise that engineer and inventor John Ericsson met Cornelius Delamater at the factory and a lasting business relationship developed from that encounter. *Scientific American* reported in Delamater's obituary, "It would have been unusual, almost unthinkable, for the Sweetish[*sic*]-American engineer to have taken the *Monitor* work anywhere else." When the Civil War broke out, Cornelius H. Delamater Ironworks was the largest marine steam-engine manufacturer in the country. It owned two hundred feet along the North River and six hundred feet fronting on Thirteenth Street and had 1,200 employees.[9]

Another New York foundry that contributed to the building of *Monitor* was Clute Brothers Foundry, which began as Clute & Bailey in Schenectady by P.I. Clute. "The foundry manufactured tools, boilers steam and caloric engines both stationary and marine for Eire Canal boats." Clute Brothers built Ericsson's caloric engines and was chosen as a subcontractor for that reason.[10]

SOUTHERN WORKS

The Selma, Alabama shipyard built the ironclads CSS *Huntsville*, CSS *Tuscaloosa* and CSS *Tennessee*, as well as having an ordnance depot. Oven Bluff, on the Tombigbee River, just sixty miles north of Mobile, left three unfinished ships when abandoned in 1862 due to an outbreak of malaria. There were shipyards in Montgomery and Mobile as well.

Located on the Yazoo River, the Yazoo City shipyard was captured early in the war. The ironclad CSS *Arkansas* was briefly stationed there when sent down from Memphis in 1861 to avoid capture.

Pensacola Navy Yard was the primary duty station for the Gulf Coast Squadron and was briefly captured by the Confederates in January 1861 and held until May 1862, when it was recaptured by the Union navy. In August 1864, just before the Battle of Mobile Bay, *Tecumseh* was in Pensacola for repairs and filled its coal bunkers before proceeding to Mobile.

Tredegar Iron Works in Richmond, Virginia, began as a small forge and rolling mill. During the war, Joseph R. Anderson's mill produced iron plate for ironclads but mainly produced cannon and ordnance for the Confederacy. The works was the largest producer of iron in the South, covering nearly five acres and employing eight hundred laborers.

Fredericksburg Shipyard was located on the Rappahannock River and produced wooden gunboats but was unable to finish their construction due to the fall of the city on December 12, 1862. Pamunky River Shipyard and York River Shipyard built wooden gunboats but also fell into Union hands in 1862.

One of the more successful shipyards was on Rocketts Landing in Richmond, producing ironclads from September 1863 to April 1865. Richmond was headquarters for the James River Squadron and produced the ironclads *Richmond*, *Fredericksburg* and *Virginia II* for the Confederate navy.

Norfolk Naval Shipyard is the oldest shipyard in the United States. It had its beginnings in 1767 as Gosport Shipyard, a private British builder until 1776. During the Civil War, it was briefly captured by the Confederacy in April 1861 and was famous for transforming the USS *Merrimack* into the CSS *Virginia*. The yard was recaptured by Union forces in May 1862.

Edward's Ferry Shipyard on the Roanoke River in North Carolina built the CSS *Albemarle* in 1862. The CSS *Neuse* was built on the Neuse River at Whitehall Shipyard, CSS *North Carolina* at Wilmington Shipyard and the CSS *Raleigh* by a private firm, Cassidy Shipyard.

Columbus Naval Iron Works in Columbus, Georgia, located on the Chattahoochee River, built CSS *Jackson*. Saffold Shipyard was also located on the Chattahoochee. Atlanta and Augusta were naval ordnance depots.

On the Mississippi River in Tennessee, the Memphis Shipyard was built in 1861 for constructing ironclads; however, it fell into Union hands when Memphis surrendered in June 1862.

It is amazing the number of ironclads that were produced in such a short period. Both North and South transformed forges, rolling mills, boiler makers and the like into facilities for building these giant war machines.

Appendix C

Tecumseh Project Phase 1 Field Operations

Table of Operations

Director NAFNAB
Smithsonian Institution

Supervisor of Salvage

General Counsel
Contracting Officer
U.S. Navy

Financial Advisor
Director of Public Affairs
Smithsonian Institution

Project Director
Field Operations

Prime Contractor
Expeditions Unlimited Inc.
Subcontractor

Administration

Cofferdam Design
   Cofferdam Construction
   Marine Salvage
   Dry Dock Services
   Others

Field Preservation Lab

Interns   Academic Volunteers   Maintenance   History & Records   Preservation

Consultants
Smithsonian Institution
U.S. Navy
Others[1]

TECUMSEH PROJECT PHASE 2 RESTORATION CENTER
MOBILE, ALABAMA

Table of Organization

Director NAFMAB
Smithsonian Institution

Director National Museums
Director Academic Programs
Smithsonian Institution

General Counsel
Director of Public Affairs
Financial Advisor
Smithsonian Institution

Contracting Officer
Smithsonian Institution

Project Director
Tecumseh Restoration Center

Administration

Conservation and Restoration

History and Office Records	Fragile Material & Small Artifacts	Ship's Hull & Hardware	Supply Maintenance	Volunteers and Security

Interns   Academics   Consultants[2]

Notes

Preface

1. McLean, USS *Alabama* Memorial Park, March 2020.
2. West, "USS *TECUMSEH*," 5.
3. Operation Tecumseh, National Archives, Washington.
4. Miller, "Dive Log and Detailed Technical Description," 27.
5. Ibid., 30–31.
6. Maury, Southern Historical Society Papers, vol. 9, 23.

Acknowledgements and Preliminary Notes

1. Maury, Southern Historical Society Papers, vol. 9, 26.
2. Ripley, *Artillery and Ammunition of the Civil War*, 99.
3. Hunter, *Year on a Monitor*.
4. Robert B. Ely, "This Filthy Ironpot," *American Heritage*, February 1958.

1. Tecumseh's First Assignment

1. Bulloch, *Secret Service of the Confederate States*, 388.
2. United States Naval War Records Office, Official Records of the Union and Confederate Navies, 399.
3. Ibid., 400.

4. Ibid.
5. Ibid., 401.
6. Ibid.
7. Ibid.
8. Ibid, 403.

2. Tecumseh *Joins the Gulf Blockading Squadron*

1. United States Naval War Records Office, *Official Records of the Union and Confederate Navies*.
2. Ibid., 567.
3. United States Naval Institute, Annapolis, Maryland.
4. Graham, *Under Both Flags*, 46.
5. United States Naval War Records Office, *Official Records of the Union and Confederate Navies*, 490–92.
6. Goodrich, "Miracle of Mobile Bay."
7. *New York Times*. "Department of the Gulf, Our Victory below Mobile."
8. Ibid., August 16, 1864.
9. Ibid.
10. Bulloch, *Secret Service of the Confederate States*, 76.

3. Torpedoes

1. Bergeron, *Confederate Mobile*, 140.
2. Von Scheliha, *Treatise on Coast-Defense*.
3. Maury, Southern Historical Society Papers, 11.
4. United States War Department, *Official Records of the Union and Confederate Armies*, 786.
5. Perry, *Infernal Machines*, 400.
6. Von Scheliha, *Treatise on Coast-Defense*.
7. Ibid.
8. Fort Macon State Park, "Hot Shot Furnace."

4. The Forts

1. Von Scheliha, *Treatise on Coast-Defense*, 17.
2. Kahler, *Regional Review*, 1.

3. Hearn, *Mobile Bay and the Mobile Campaign*, 45.
4. United States Naval War Records Office, *Official Records of the Union and Confederate Navies*, 520.
5. Ibid., 521.

5. Personal Observations

1. "A Voice from the Past," *Mobile Press*.
2. "Fort Morgan in the Confederacy," *Alabama Historical Quarterly*.
3. Smith, *Two Naval Journals*, 4–5.
4. Tarpley, *When Duty Calls: The Civil War Diary of Sergeant Robert B. Tarpley*.
5. Ebson C. Lambert, *Civil War Diary*, "Battle of Mobile Bay." Special Collections, University of Alabama Archives.
6. Alabama Department of Archives and History, Box# SPR425, Joseph Wilkinson.
7. Jones, *Civil War at Sea*, 249.
8. "Percival Drayton," Wikipedia, www.Wikipedia.org.
9. Ibid.
10. Ibid.
11. Smith, *Two Naval Journals*, 43.
12. "Damning Torpedoes for Four Hours," *Daybook*, 5.
13. *New York Times*, August 13, 1864.
14. United States War Department, *Official Records of the Union and Confederate Armies*, 226–27.

6. Commander Profiles

1. "John Ericsson," National Park Service.
2. "Monitor Center," Mariners' Museum and Park.
3. "Gideon Welles," Wikipedia.
4. Ibid.
5. Ibid.
6. Friend, *West Wind, Flood Tide*, 245.
7. American Battlefield Trust, "David G. Farragut."
8. Fort Morgan Historic Site, "Private Robert B. Tarpley."
9. United States War Department, *Official Records of the Union and Confederate Armies*, Series L, Volume 29, Part 2, 344.

10. Ibid., 390.

11. Bulloch, *Secret Service of the Confederate States*, 205–6.

12. "Franklin Buchanan," Wikipedia.

13. Ibid.

14. "Dabney H. Maury," Wikipedia.

15. "Dabney Herndon Maury," Encyclopedia Virginia.

16. Ibid.

17. "Stephen Russell Mallory," Wikipedia.

18. Ibid.

7. Newspaper Press Reports

1. Lee, "Bay Searched for Trace," *Mobile Press*.

2. Sellers, "Secret of Tecumseh Revealed," *Mobile Press*.

3. Ed Lee, *Mobile Press Register*, February 19, 1967.

4. "Tecumseh Suit Hearing," *Mobile Press*.

5. Ibid.

6. McDonnell, "War for Tecumseh Opens," *Mobile Press*.

7. *Mobile Press*, March 26, 1967.

8. Lee, "Case of Ironclad Tecumseh," *Mobile Press*.

9. Lee, "Ship Salvage in News Now," *Mobile Press Register*.

10. "Can't Move Tecumseh," *Press Capital Bureau*.

11. Ibid.

12. "Fight Rages on Ironclad," *Mobile Press*.

13. Lee, "Cairo Saga Might Be Text," *Mobile Press Register*.

14. "Fight Rages on Ironclad," *Mobile Press*.

15. Friend, *Preliminary Considerations*.

8. 1967 Smithsonian Institution Survey and Dive Notes

1. West, *USS Tecumseh Shipwreck Management Plan*, 29–30.

2. National Armed Forces Museum Advisory Board, *USS Tecumseh*, 12.

3. Ibid., 5.

4. Miller, "Dive Log and Detailed Technical Description," 1–2.

5. Ibid., 1–99.

6. West, *USS Tecumseh Shipwreck Management Plan*, 29.

7. Miller, "Dive Log and Detailed Technical Description," 1–2, July 7, 1967.

8. Ibid., 3–8, July 8.

9. Ibid., 9–11, July 9.
10. Ibid., 12–17, July 11.
11. Ibid., 18–21, July 12.
12. Ibid., 22–31, July 13.
13. Ibid., 32–36, July 14.
14. Ibid., 37–46, July 15.
15. Ibid., 47–51, July 16.
16. Ibid., 52–58, July 17.
17. Ibid., 59–67, July 18.
18. Ibid., 68–74, July 19.
19. Ibid., 75–80, July 20.
20. Ibid., 81–88, July 21.
21. Ibid., 89–92, July 22.
22. Ibid., 93–99, July 23.

9. Recovered Artifacts

1. National Armed Forces Museum Advisory Board, *USS Tecumseh*, November 25, 1968.
2. Ibid.

10. Subsequent Surveys

1. West, *USS Tecumseh Shipwreck Management Plan*, 34.
2. West, "USS *TECUMSEH*," 109.
3. Ibid., 109.
4. Ibid.
5. Ibid.
6. Ibid., 35.
7. Ibid., 36.
8. Ibid., 37.
9. Ibid., 41.
10. Schell, Alabama Gulf Coast Archaeological Society, 1977 Survey, 2.
11. Ibid., 5
12. West, *USS Tecumseh Shipwreck Management Plan*, 42.
13. Ibid., 42–43.
14. Watts, *Mobile Bay Shipwreck Survey*, 53–55.

15. Ibid.
16. Interview with Alabama state archaeologist Stacey Hathorne, 2020.

11. Other Salvage Attempts

1. *Mobile Press Register*, November 20, 1957.
2. Department of Defense, Legacy Recourse Management Program, 7–8.
3. Ibid.

Summary and Conclusions

1. Neyland, *Sovereign Immunity and the Management of United States Naval Shipwrecks*, 104–9.
2. *Mobile Press Register*, unknown date.

Appendix A

1. United States Naval War Records Office, *Official Records of the Union and Confederate Navies*, 401–93.
2. Emily Hosmer, personal correspondence, Covington, Louisiana, March 1967.

Appendix B

1. Still, *Monitor Builders*, 8.
2. Morrison, *History of American Steam Navigation*.
3. Still, *Monitor Builders*, 8.
4. Ibid.
5. Ibid., 9.
6. Ibid.
7. Ibid., 11.
8. Ibid., 14.
9. Ibid., 18.
10. Ibid., 22.

Appendix C

1. Wilson, *USS Tecumseh Shipwreck Management Plan*, Appendix 2, 33.
2. Ibid., 34.

Bibliography

Government Sources

Alabama Department of Archives and History. Box# SPR425. Joseph Wilkinson, Personal Diary. Montgomery, Alabama.

———. *Diary of the Siege of Fort Morgan, August 5, 1864.* First Lieutenant Joseph Biddle Wilkinson, First Tennessee Heavy Artillery. Montgomery, Alabama.

Department of the Army. Mobile District. Corps of Engineers. Personal correspondence.

Department of Defense. Legacy Resource Management Program. Project (94-1704), 1996.

Fort Macon State Park. "Hot Shot Furnace." Atlantic Beach, North Carolina.

Fort Morgan Historic Site. Mobile Point. "Private Robert B. Tarpley." First Tennessee, Heavy Artillery, Diary, July 4 to September 15, 1864.

General Service Administration. "Operation Tecumseh, Mobile, Alabama, 7 July–23 July, 1967." Washington, D.C.

Hampton Roads Naval Museum. Department of the Navy. "Damning Torpedoes for Four Hours: Three Views of Mobile Bay (1864)." *The Daybook, Civil War Navy.* Special Edition.

Mariners' Museum and Park. Newport News, Virginia.

Mobile Public Library. Local History Division. Mobile, Alabama.

National Armed Forces Museum Advisory Board. *USS Tecumseh: Capsule of History.* James J. Stokesberry. Washington, D.C.: Smithsonian Institution, 1969.

National Museum of the United States Army. Fort Belvoir, Virginia.

National Oceanic and Atmospheric Administration. Office of Coast Survey.

National Park Service. www.nps.gov.htm.

National Park Service. *Regional Review* 2, no. 2 (February 1939).

Naval Historical Collection. USS *Tecumseh* File. Knox to Dowling, June 29, 1938.

Naval Research Laboratory. *Examination of the Corrosion and Salt Contamination of Structural Metal from the USS TECUMSEH.* Washington, D.C., March 1969.

Smithsonian Institution Archives. Tecumseh Project photos. Box 11 RU 581. Washington, D.C. Deborah Shapiro.

Smithsonian Institution Investigations. Buster Miller Files. July 7–23, 1967.

Smithsonian Institution. *Detailed Description of the Monitor USS Tecumseh Report.* Washington, D.C.

———. United States National Museum. Washington, D.C., *C.A. Laboratory Report*, February 7, 1974.

United States Army Combined Arms Center. *Operational Art and the Campaigns for Mobile, 1864–65: A Staff Ride Handbook.* Fort Leavenworth, KS: Combat Studies Institute Press, 2019.

United States Department of Commerce. NOAA and Marine and Estuarine Management. Washington, D.C. William N. Still Jr., 1988

United States General Services Administration. National Archives and Records Service. Personal correspondence.

United States Naval Institute. Annapolis, Maryland.

United States Naval Undersea Museum. Keyport, Washington. Mary Ryan, curator.

United States Naval War Records Office. Official Records of the Union and Confederate Navies in the War of the Rebellion. Series I, Volume 21, Operations: West Gulf Blockading. January 1 to December 31, 1864. Washington, D.C.: Government Printing Office, 1894.

United States War College Review 54, no. 1 (Winter 2001).

United States War Department. Official Records of the Union and Confederate Armies. Series I, Volume 39, Part II, May 1864–September, 1864. Washington, D.C.: Government Printing Office, 1894.

Washington Navy Yard, Washington, D.C. Clayton Farrington.

West, W. Wilson, Jr. *USS Tecumseh Shipwreck Management Plan.* Department of Defense Legacy Resource Management Program. Naval Historical Center. The National Maritime Initiative, National Park Service and National Conference of State Historic Preservation Officers, 1997.

Periodicals

Baldwin, H.D. "Farragut in Mobile Bay, Recollections of One Who Took Part in the Battle." *Scribner's Monthly* X, no. 111 (February 1877).

Durham, Frances. "Eastern Shores Echoes." *Mobile (AL) Press*, April 21, 1967.

Encyclopedia Virginia. "Dabney Herndon Maury." www.encyclopediavirginia.org.

Felder, James. "Much Learned on Tecumseh after 4 Days of Dive." *Mobile Press*, July 11, 1967, 1 and 6.

"Fort Morgan in the Confederacy." *Alabama Historical Quarterly* 7, no. 2 (Spring 1944): 254–68.

Goodrich, Casper S. "The Miracle of Mobile Bay." *Deseret Evening News*, August 29, 1910.

Hammer, Roger. "Tecumseh May Stay." *Mobile Press*, August 10, 1967.

Harper's Weekly, "Fort Morgan and the Rebel Fleet." 8, no. 399 (August 20, 1864).

———, May 7, 1862; February 13, 1864.

Jackson, Guy L. "Naval Warfare Modernized by Battle of Mobile Bay." *Mobile Press Register (AL)*, August 6, 1967.

Kahler, Herbert E. *The Regional Review* 2, no. 2 (February 1939). National Park Service.

Lee, Ed. "Bay Searched for Trace of Union Ship Tecumseh." *Mobile Press,* January 12, 1967, 1 and 6.

———. "Cairo Saga Might Be Text for Decision on Tecumseh." *Mobile Press Register*, April 2, 1967, 1.

———. "Case of Ironclad Tecumseh Transferred to U.S Court." *Mobile Press*, March 25, 1967.

———. "Ship Salvage in News Now; Bulletin Gives Few Points." *Mobile Press Register*, March 26, 1967, 11-A.

———. "With Tecumseh Upside Down, What Is That Tower Thing?" *Mobile Press Register*, February 19, 1967, 3-B.

Manuppelli, Tony, "Search For Civil War Ship." *Mobile Press,* January 12, 1967.

McDonnell, Harry. "Admiral Lauds Tecumseh Project." *Mobile Press* (undated).

———. "New Study Slated on Raising Ironclad Tecumseh." *Mobile Press*, January 17, 1974.

———. "War for Tecumseh Opens." *Mobile Press*, March 16, 1967.

Mitchell, Garry. "Tecumseh May Stay in Mobile Bay Grave." *Mobile Press*, June 16, 1983.

Mobile Press. "And the Tecumseh." February 1967.

————. "Clearance Seen for Tecumseh." May 30, 1969.

————. "Court Refuses Suit." April 3, 1967.

————. "Fight Rages on Ironclad." March 28, 1967, 1 and 3.

————. "Georgia Turned Down for Ironclad Tecumseh." May 1, 1968.

————. "Graves Offered Tecumseh Dead." July 24, 1967.

————. "Jaycees File Ship Protest." March 16, 1967, 1-B

————. "Jaycees Get Salvage Nod." March 16, 1967, 1 and 8.

————. "Let Mobilians See Tecumseh." July 27, 1967.

————. "Officials Stumped on How to Raise Union Ironclad Tecumseh." May 26, 1969.

————. "Smithsonian Alters Plan on Tecumseh." July 9, 1969.

————. "Smithsonian Institute Delays Tecumseh Lift." April 10, 1970.

————. "Smithsonian Officials 'Optimistic' on Raising Tecumseh in October." August 2, 1968.

————. "Smithsonian Seeking to Salvage Tecumseh." March 1967.

————. "Sunken Ironclad's Anchor Raised." July 22, 1967, 1 and 8.

————. "Tecumseh Anchor Raising Slated Sometime Today." July 21, 1967.

————. "Tecumseh Anchor Recovered." July 22, 1967.

————. "Tecumseh Guns Had 'Last Word' in Bay Battle." February 24, 1974.

————. "Tecumseh Hull Said Damaged by Torpedo." July 18, 1967.

————. "Tecumseh in Fine Shape." August 29, 1967, 1 and 6.

————. "Tecumseh Job Starts August 1." July 9, 1969.

————. "Tecumseh Job Starts Aug. 1." July 28, 1967.

————. "Tecumseh Suit Hearing Date Expected Today." March 10, 1967.

————. "2 Year Task Is Predicted on Iron." August 5, 1967, 1.

————. "A Voice from the Past." July 21, 2006.

————. "Won't Give Up the Battleship." May 18, 1967, 1 and 8.

Mobile Press Register. "Smithsonian Institute Delays Tecumseh Lift." April 10, 1970.

————. "State Moves to Stake Out Claim to Union Ironclad in Bay Here." March 12, 1967.

New York Times. "Department of the Gulf: A Monitor Sunk by a Torpedo." April 21, 1967.

————. "The Department of the Gulf, Our Victory below Mobile: A Dispatch from Gen. Banks, a Monitor Sunk by Torpedo." August 13, 1864.

Press Capitol Bureau (Montgomery AL). "Can't Move Tecumseh." March 27, 1967, 1 and 6.

Richey, B.J. "Officials Stumped On How To Raise Union Ironclad Tecumseh." *Mobile Press*, May 26, 1969.

Sellers, Bill. "Secret of Tecumseh Revealed." *Mobile Press*, February 18, 1967.

Books

Anderson, Bern. *By Sea and By River, the Naval History of the Civil War*. New York: Da Capo Press, 1962.

Bergeron, Arthur W., Jr. *Confederate Mobile*. Jackson: University Press of Mississippi, 1991.

Bulloch, James D. *The Secret Service of the Confederate States in Europe*. Vol. 2. New York, G.P. Putnam's Sons, 1959.

Coombie, Jack D. *Gunfire Around the Gulf, the Last Major Campaigns of the Civil War*. New York: Bantam Books, 1999.

deKay, James Tertius. *MONITOR: The Story of the Legendary Civil War Ironclad and the Man Whose Invention Changed the Course of History*. New York: Ballantine Books, 1997.

Delaney, Caldwell. *The Story of Mobile*. Mobile, AL: HB Publications, Haunted Book Shop, 1981.

Friend, Jack. *West Wind, Flood Tide: The Battle of Mobile Bay*. Annapolis, MD: Naval Institute Press, 2004.

Graham, C.R. *Under Both Flags*. Baltimore, MD: R.H. Woodward Company, 1896.

Hearn, Chester G. *Mobile Bay and the Mobile Campaign*. Jefferson, NC: McFarland & Company, 1993.

Hoehling, A.A. *Damn the Torpedoes, Naval Incidents of the Civil War*. Winston-Salem, NC: John F. Blair, 1989

Hunter, Alvah Folsom. *A Year on a Monitor and the Destruction of Fort Sumter*. Columbia: University of South Carolina Press, 1991.

Johnson, Robert Underwood, and Clarence Clough Buel, eds. *Battles and Leaders of the Civil War*. Vol. 4. New York: Century Company, 1888.

Jones, Virgil Carrington. *The Civil War at Sea*. Vol. 3. New York: Holt, Rinehart and Winston, 1961.

Maury, Dabney H. Southern Historical Society Papers. Vol. 3, January to June 1877.

Miller, F.T., ed. *The Photographic History of the Civil War*. Vol. 6. New York: Review of Reviews Company, 1911.

Morrison, John H. *History of American Steam Navigation*. New York: W.F. Sametz and Company, 1903.

Musicant, Ivan. *Divided Waters: The Naval History of the Civil War*. Edison, NJ: Castle Books, 2000.

Nash, Howard P., Jr. *A Naval History of the Civil War*. Cranbury, NJ: A.S. Barnes and Company, 1972.

Nelson, James L. *Reign of Iron, the Story of the First Battling Ironclads: The* Monitor *and the* Merrimack. New York: Harper Collins Publishers, 2004.

Niven, John. *Gideon Welles, Lincoln's Secretary of the Navy*. New York: Oxford University Press, 1973.

Perry, Milton F. *Infernal Machines, the Story of Confederate Submarine and Mine Warfare*. Baton Rouge: Louisiana State University Press, 1985.

Quarstein, John V. *A History of Ironclads: The Power of Iron over Wood*. Charleston, SC: The History Press, 2006.

Ripley, Warren. *Artillery and Ammunition of the Civil War*. New York: Promontory Press, 1970.

Roberts, William H. *Civil War Ironclads, the U.S. Navy and Industrial Mobilization*. Baltimore. MD: Johns Hopkins Press, 2002.

Smith, C. Carter. *Two Naval Journals: 1864, at the Battle of Mobile Bay*. Chicago: Wyvern Press, 1964.

Southern Historical Society Papers. *Civil War Times Illustrated*. New York: Kraus Reprint Company, 1977.

Still, William N., Jr. *Confederate Shipbuilding*. Athens: University of Georgia Press, 1969.

————. *Iron Afloat: The Story of the Confederate Ironclads*. Nashville, TN: Vanderbilt University Press, 1971.

————. *Monitor Builders: A Historical Study of the Principal Firms and Individuals Involved in the Construction of USS* Monitor. Washington, D.C.: National Maritime Initiative, 1988.

Von Scheliha, Victor. *A Treatise on Coast-Defense*. London: E. & F.N. Spon, 1868.

Letters, Diaries, Private Publications and Correspondence

Alabama Historical Quarterly, summer, 1945, Volume 7, number 2. "Fort Morgan in the Confederacy."

Ames, Dan. *A Brief Summary of Recent Investigations on USS Tecumseh*. 1977.

Arbuckle, Alex Q. *the Strange But Deadly Ironclad Ships of the Civil War*.

Beeson, Nick, History Museum of Mobile, Alabama. Personal correspondence.

East Carolina University. Department of Maritime History and Nautical Archaeology. Greenville, North Carolina.

Friend, Jack. *Preliminary Considerations: The Salvage, Preservation and Display of USS Tecumseh Report.* June 1994.

Hathorne, Stacey, State of Alabama Archaeologist, Alabama Historical Commission. Personal correspondence.

Holcombe, Bob, Confederate navy historian. Personal correspondence.

Hosmer, Emily. Personal correspondence,

Lambert, Esbon C. *A Civil War Diary: Life in 1863–1864 for a Union Sailor on the Gunboat USS* Itasca *during the Battle of Mobile Bay.* Personal diary.

Louis J. Cupozzoli & Associates, consulting engineers. *Engineer Drawings of Proposed Cofferdam around the Tecumseh.* Baldwin County, Alabama, 1967.

McLean, Shea W., curator. USS *Alabama* Memorial Park. Mobile, Alabama.

Miller, Buster. "Dive Log and Detailed Technical Description of the Monitor USS Tecumseh Report July 7 to July 23, 1967."

Mobile Junior Chamber of Commerce. Mobile, Alabama. Personal correspondence, 1967.

Neyland, Robert S. "Sovereign Immunity and the Management of United States Naval Shipwrecks." Society for Historical Archaeology, *Underwater Archaeology*, 1996.

Saltus, Allen, underwater archaeologist. Personal correspondence.

Schell, Sidney H., Alabama Gulf Coast Archaeological Society Inc. 1977 Survey.

Tarpley, Robert B. *When Duty Calls: The Civil War Diary of Sergeant Robert B. Tarpley, 1861–1865.* Box: 1, Folder: 1. Frank M. Hodgson Collection, 2004.003. Montgomery County (TN) Archives.

Watts, Gordon P., Jr. *Mobile Bay Shipwreck Survey*, 1994.

———. *Toward Establishing Research and Significance Criteria for Civil War Shipwreck Resources.* Society for Historical Archaeology, Tucson, 1998.

West, W. Wilson, Jr. "The USS *TECUMSEH*." Thesis, Department of History, East Carolina University, June 1985.

Index

A

Alabama Militia 55
Alabama River 68
Anderson, General Charles 54
Armistead, William R. 112
artillery 36, 52, 53
Augusta 29, 30
Austill, Confederate Second
    Lieutenant Hurieosco 58

B

Banks, General Nathaniel 66
battle damage 91, 94, 95, 96
Bienville 30, 31
Blakeley River 45, 47
Brooklyn 21, 37, 59, 61
Brooklyn, 37
Brother, Private Charles 61
Buchanan, Commander Franklin 33

buoys 40
Bushnell, David 48

C

Canby, General E.R.S. 55
cofferdam 102
Columbaid 53
Cottrell, Acting Master Gardner 39

D

Dahlgerns 37
Dahlgren 21
Dauphin Island 30, 49, 54, 55, 85
Davidson, Lieutenant Hunter 44
divers 60, 83, 84, 96, 110, 112, 115
dive team 84
dredge 88

E

Ericsson, John 20, 63, 64, 69
Espy, Huston & Associates 112
Evening Star 41

F

Farragut, David 17, 29, 30, 31, 36, 37, 38, 41, 44, 45, 54, 55, 56, 60, 66, 68, 69, 70
First Alabama Battery 58
floating battery 49
Fort Gaines 49, 54, 55, 56, 59
Fort Morgan 9, 20, 23, 36, 37, 39, 45, 49, 52, 53, 55, 56, 57, 58, 59, 61, 68, 70, 73
Fort Powell 49, 54, 56
Fretwell, J.R. 43

G

Gaines, General Edmund Pendleton 54
Gibson, Lieutenant Commander Alexander 30
Grant's Pass 49
Gulf Blockading Squadron 35

H

Hartford 30, 37, 40, 56, 59, 60, 61, 66, 69
hatch 60, 68, 91, 98, 99
hot shot furnace 52

I

ironclad 27, 49, 58, 60, 63, 69, 70, 74, 75, 76, 77, 81, 110
Itasca 59
Ivanhoe 61

J

Jouett 38

L

Lackawanna 60
Lambert, Landsman Ebson C. 59
Langley, C.F. 40

M

magazines 25, 54, 57
Mahopac 20
Mallory, Stephen Russell 71
Manhattan 20, 36
Maury, Dabney 70
Metacomet 31, 38, 39, 61
mines 43, 44, 48, 92
Mobile Point 9, 36, 49, 112
Mobile River 47
monitor 20, 27, 33, 36, 37, 41, 47, 49, 55, 56, 58, 60, 65, 68, 74, 83, 84, 109

N

National Armed Forces Museum Advisory 81
National Armed Forces Museum Park 78, 81
National Geographic 85, 96, 97
Naval Submarine Battery Service 44
Neilds, Ensign H.C. 38
New Orleans 41, 44, 56, 57, 58, 66, 68, 87

O

obstructions 47, 65
O'Connell, John C. 58
Operation Tecumseh 84
Ossipee 59

P

Pensacola Bay 29
Philippi 61
pilot 21, 25, 33, 37, 38, 39, 59, 60, 68
pilothouse 22, 38, 60
Port Royal 29, 31, 54
Potomac 30

R

Rains, General Gabriel J. 43, 44
Red River campaign 44
Richmond 30, 31, 61, 70, 72
rudder 88, 89, 91, 92, 94

S

salvage 74, 75, 76, 82, 84, 87, 94, 97, 109, 110, 126
Schell, Sidney H. 112
Singer, E.C. 43
Smithsonian Institution 23, 74, 76, 77, 81, 84, 99, 110, 112, 142
speaking tube 22, 37
Stimers, Alban C. 65
survivors 40

T

Tennessee 17, 31, 33, 37, 41, 56, 58, 59, 60, 70, 71
Tensas River 68
torpedo 37, 41, 43, 44, 47, 48, 55, 56, 59, 61, 65, 68, 84, 91, 93, 97
Tunis A. M. Graven 33
Tunis Augustus Macdonough Craven 27
turret 21, 25, 37, 38, 39, 58, 60, 68, 83, 86, 91, 92, 93, 95, 96, 99, 110
Twenty-First Alabama Infantry Regiment 54

V

Von Scheliha, Viktor 49

W

warships 36
Welles, Gideon 60, 64, 65

Whiting, Captain Julian Wythe
    (J.W.) 57
Williams, Lt. Colonel James W. 54
Winnebago 36

About the Author

D avid Smithweck is a graduate of Spring Hill College in Mobile, Alabama, a Civil War historian, and for over fifty years he has participated in projects such as the search and identification of two Confederate ironclad gunboats, CSS *Huntsville* and CSS *Tuscaloosa*, in the Mobile River; the investigation and mapping of Fort Powell in Mississippi Sound; investigations of the Civil War works at Oven Bluff and Choctaw Bluff on the Alabama and Tombigbee Rivers; and the Confederate obstructions in upper Mobile Bay.

David served four three-year terms on the board of directors of the Mobile History Museum, was on the board of directors of the Alabama Lighthouse Association and founded the Alabama Gulf Coast Archaeological Society Inc. in 1977.